Jesus

A Gospel

Other Orbis Books by Henri Nouwen

Adam: God's Beloved

Desert Wisdom: Sayings from the Desert Fathers
(with Yushi Nomura)

¡Gracias! A Latin American Journal

Henri Nouwen, Writings Selected with an
Introduction by Robert A. Jonas

The Road to Peace: Writings on Peace and Justice

Walk with Jesus: Stations of the Cross

With Burning Hearts:
 A Meditation on the Eucharistic Life

⁂ *Jesus* ⁂
A Gospel

HENRI NOUWEN

Edited and Introduced by Michael O'Laughlin

ORBIS BOOKS
Maryknoll, New York 10545

Founded in 1970, Orbis Books endeavors to publish works that enlighten the mind, nourish the spirit, and challenge the conscience. The publishing arm of Maryknoll Fathers and Brothers, Orbis seeks to explore the global dimensions of the Christian faith and mission, to invite dialogue with diverse cultures and religious traditions, and to serve the cause of reconciliation and peace. The books published reflect the views of their authors and do not represent the official position of the Society.

To obtain more information about Maryknoll and Orbis Books, please visit our website at www.orbisbooks.com

Published by Orbis Books, Maryknoll, NY 10545-0308.
Designed by Roberta Savage.

Manufactured in the United States of America

Library of Congress Cataloging-in-Publication Data
Nouwen, Henri J. M.
 Jesus: a gospel/Henri Nouwen; edited and introduced by Michael O'Laughlin.
  p. cm.
 Includes bibliographical references and index.
 ISBN 978-1-57075-384-8(cloth); 978-1-62698-014-3(pbk)
 1. Jesus Christ—Biography—Meditations. 2. Bible. N.T. Gospels—Meditations. I. O'Laughlin, Michael. II. title.

BT306.43 .N68 2001
232.9'01—dc21
[B]
                                                         2001036155

The whole message of the Gospel is this:

Become like Jesus.

—Bread for the Journey

Contents

Death and Darkness Are Overcome

Jesus, A Gospel

Acknowledgements

One of the pleasures of editing a book by Henri Nouwen is being in contact with the handful of wonderful people who have shaped Henri's legacy through their writing and organizational efforts. I owe a great deal to these friends; sometimes I was able to consult their books and they helped me without them even realizing they had done so. Therefore, first of all, let me thank all of Henri's friends, especially the writers and editors, who have kept his spirit alive and well. Special thanks are due to Sue Mosteller, director of the Henri Nouwen Literary Centre, for her efforts to preserve Henri's legacy and help it grow and mature. I also want to give thanks to those who have created anthologies of Henri's work and who gave me help and encouragement: Robert Durback, editor of *Seeds of Hope*, Wendy Greer, editor of *The Only Necessary Thing*, and especially my friend and neighbor, Robert Jonas, who created the Henri Nouwen volume for the Orbis Modern Spiritual Masters series.

The person who contributed the most to the conception and production of this book is Robert Ellsberg, editor in chief of Orbis Books. As an editor he successfully traversed the line between being overly supportive and overly critical of me and was always friendly and generous. I also want to thank Catherine Costello, the production manager, for her efforts to get this book in shape. Thanks to Roberta Savage, who gave the book its artistic design, its layout and its cover. Finally, I would like to thank Paul Gormley for his help and advice early on concerning computer issues and for putting his office equipment at my disposal on many occasions.

Many thanks to all.

Michael O'Laughlin

Permissions

Acknowledgment is gratefully made to the following publishers for permission to reprint excerpts from the works of Henri J.M. Nouwen:

Ave Maria Press, PO Box 428, Notre Dame, IN 46556, www.avemariapress.com, for *Behold the Beauty of the Lord*, copyright © 1987; *Can You Drink the Cup? The Challenge of the Spiritual Life*, copyright © 1996. Used by permission of Ave Maria Press.

Crossroad Publishing Company for *Here and Now*, copyright © 1994; *In the Name of Jesus: Reflections on Christian Leadership*, copyright © 1989; *The Life of the Beloved*, copyright © 1992; *Sabbatical Journey: The Final Year*, copyright © 1998. All copyrights by Henri J.M. Nouwen. Reprinted by permission of The Crossroad Publishing Company. www.crossroadpublishing.com.

Doubleday, a division of Random House, Inc. for *Clowning in Rome*, copyright © 1979; *A Cry for Mercy*, copyright © 1981; *The Inner Voice of Love*, copyright © 1996; *Lifesigns: Intimacy, Fecundity and Ecstasy in Christian Perspective*, copyright © 1986; *Reaching Out*, copyright © 1975; *The Return of the Prodigal Son* copyright © 1992; *The Road to Daybreak: A Spiritual Journey*, copyright © 1988. All copyrights by Henri J.M. Nouwen. Used by permission of Doubleday, a division of Random House, Inc.

HarperCollins Publishers for *Bread for the Journey*, copyright © 1997; *Letters to Marc about Jesus*, copyright © 1988; *The Living Reminder: Service and Prayer in Memory of Jesus Christ*, copyright © 1977;

Making All Things New: An Invitation to the Spiritual Life, copyright © 1981; *Our Greatest Gift: A Meditation on Dying and Caring*, copyright © 1994. Reprinted by permission of HarperCollins Publishers.

L'Arche Daybreak Community for *Living the Beatitudes*, copyright © 1989 by the L'Arche Daybreak Community.

Excerpts from *The New Jerusalem Bible*, copyright © 1985 by Doubleday, a division of Random House, Inc. and Darton, Longman & Todd Ltd., used by permission of the publishers.

"Parting Words: A Conversation on Prayer with Henri Nouwen," interviewed by Rebecca Laird in *Sacred Journey: The Journal of Fellowship in Prayer*, no. 6, December 1996. Reprinted with permission of *Sacred Journey*.

Darton, Longman & Todd Ltd., for excerpts from the following works copyrighted in the United Kingdom: *Here and Now*, copyright © 1994; *Clowning in Rome*, copyright © 1979; *The Return of the Prodigal Son*, copyright © 1992; *In the Name of Jesus*, copyright © 1989; *The Inner Voice of Love*, copyright © 1996. Reprinted by permission of Darton, Longman & Todd Ltd.

The Henri Nouwen Legacy Trust for permission to reprint additional texts by Henri J.M. Nouwen.

Introduction

Should you choose to read it, this book can guide you along new pathways through the Gospel. This is not a journey that you must take alone: the best Christian experiences are seldom solitary ones! Your guide on the journey will be Henri Nouwen, the most influential and beloved of modern Christian writers on spirituality. As you move through this familiar but ever-surprising landscape, I am confident that the message of Jesus will sound a new note within you. Henri Nouwen had a unique ability to find new, deeper meaning in the Gospel and open the hearts of his readers to its message about Jesus and themselves.

I know this because I saw it happen many times: I first met Henri at Harvard University, where he taught spirituality and I was his teaching fellow. I remember vividly how the lecture hall overflowed with students when Henri taught his classes. I remember how tears came to the eyes of a number of his listeners—an unusual sight at Harvard—and I remember how great an impact those classes had on everyone. Henri had a way of making the Gospel come alive. He made us conscious of who we are and where we were at that moment. He made us aware of all that was going on in the world and what the Gospel had to say about our world and our lives.

Henri created for us a sense of spiritual community. He taught us by example, and not only with words. In one of his bolder moves, he even had us send a "delegation" from our number to spend their spring break in Haiti. The class also raised a huge amount of money for supplies to be distributed in the missions in Haiti. We also wrote spiritual journals, and gave and received spiritual direction. In the end it didn't feel like a class, it felt like it was an invitation to experience real Christianity.

By the time Henri taught at Harvard he was an Ivy League veteran. He had spent ten years teaching at Yale.

Those were the tumultuous years of the Civil Rights movement and the Vietnam war. By the time I met him, he had already become famous in Christian circles as a bold spiritual pioneer. He had marched with Martin Luther King, spent long months in the silence of a Cistercian monastery, and done missionary work in South America. He was also enjoying growing popularity as a writer. His books were in a more psychological vein at first, but then they turned more and more to Henri's unique perspective on the Bible, the sacraments and the core of Christian experience.

Henri possessed the rare gift of being able to speak in simple terms. In fact, he came to Harvard very much in the spirit of St. Paul, who decided not to clothe his message in a persuasive display of learning; Paul said his intent was to talk about Jesus, pure and simple, and I think Henri was attempting to do the same. He certainly did not deal with the intellectuals of Harvard on their own terms; instead, he spoke to the heart, and he focused what he had to say on Jesus.

Jesus is the most revered figure in the Western world. His life and his teaching are stamped deeply into the fabric of our psychology and our history. Yet Jesus remains a mystery. There is an empty space for many, perhaps for most of us, in that inner place where we are supposed to meet and embrace the Lord of all. Many feel a sense of disappointment when it comes to Jesus; perhaps they just want to "experience more" of the power and presence of the man whom death could not hold.

It is such a common feeling . . . I think most of us can identify with the man in the Gospel who was questioned by Jesus about faith. He answered, "Lord, I have faith. Help my lack of faith!" (Mark 9:24). When it comes to Jesus, we are all very much like that man. We have faith, but we wish we had more. Perhaps we do know Jesus, but we long to know him better.

In any event, we go on. Every once in a while we hear about some place or some situation where God seemed to suddenly make an impact. These stories are inspiring for us, especially since they seem to defy our expectations. The Spirit of Jesus, that holy and fiery wind, suddenly blows where we least expect! But there is a question in our hearts, one that we are usually unwilling to voice: might that wind blow our way and touch us? The answer to this question is, "Yes."

The way the Spirit touches us may not be so mysterious after all. What the early church called "the good news" was often communicated by one person reaching out to another person. There has always been a place in Christianity for the teacher. We need teachers to bring us closer to God; sometimes that is how the Spirit reaches us and touches us. We need teachers not merely to show us the way we should live, but to explain for us God's special way of doing things—those faint and far-from-obvious signs that God is caring for us and our world. This is what Henri Nouwen did—he was a teacher, a man sent from God, and his ministry was to show people like us what God is doing in the world and how we might respond.

I think this book might be more helpful to you than many others you might read. I have read, heard speak, and even known personally many well-known interpreters of the Bible. However, I must say that my contact with most of these famous teachers has been tinged with a measure of disappointment. There have been fairly few that I could trust or admire without reservation. In most cases, their lives did not seem to be much affected by their Christian faith. Although I could admire their great learning, they didn't seem to truly believe or accept the Gospel's message. Only one of them chose to follow Jesus wherever he led; only one gave himself to spreading the good news and living in the Spirit, instead of living a scholarly existence in some university library. That one special teacher was Henri Nouwen.

Henri stayed at Harvard only two years. He didn't feel at home there, and even became depressed to the point of crisis. Henri was waiting for God to speak to him, to reveal to him where he should be and what he should be doing.

Henri was waiting for a "call." This is always an intense and fearsome undertaking. When a call did come for Henri, it was to begin something he never would have imagined doing—he was asked to become the chaplain at Daybreak, the L'Arche community in Toronto, Canada. L'Arche is an ecumenical faith community that gives young people the opportunity to live in community with the handicapped. There are L'Arche houses all over the world. However, even though L'Arche is so international, it is a small group—a small, hidden expression of God's way in the world.

The L'Arche experience transformed Henri completely. Henri was someone who needed a lot of love, and at Daybreak he experienced some of the love he needed. Although it was a loving community, Henri also found Daybreak to be a disarming, unsettling place. His lifestyle and assumptions were fundamentally challenged. A man of words, he suddenly found himself among people who could not understand words. A man of action, he suddenly found himself among people who could not move their bodies. He was profoundly affected by the vulnerability of those around him.

Then something miraculous happened: The great teacher found that these wounded and handicapped people had become his teachers. Even Adam, who was unable to move about, to speak, or even to make eye contact, was communicating something to Henri, and so was the Holy Spirit. The neediness and vulnerability of the handicapped was the occasion of great intimacy and affection. Henri listened and he learned. The New Testament now had new meaning for Henri. It was at L'Arche that many of Henri Nouwen's greatest insights into the Gospel emerged. Here he wrote some of his finest books. His message became yet again more simple, and more focused on Jesus.

Henri remained at Daybreak for ten years. His death in 1996 came about in a way which, sad as it was, seemed fitting to me: Henri had written one of his best books about Rembrandt's painting, The Return of the Prodigal Son, a book so moving that Hillary Clinton said it was the one book she would recommend to those "going through difficult times in their lives." She had read it during her darkest hours in the White House.

Henri was asked to go to St. Petersburg, in Russia, where the painting hangs, to do a television film about his book. He made a stopover in his native Holland to meet the film crew. He checked into a hotel there to rest, and and became very ill. He had had a sudden heart attack. His family rushed to be with him, as did his closest friends from Canada. At first Henri was in great pain, and made preparations for death. Then he seemed to get better. Within a couple of days he was walking around. Then a second heart attack came and he died.

I take solace in the fact that Henri returned to Holland, returned to his family, and returned to Rembrandt's painting as part of his return to God. For his burial he even returned to Daybreak. He died and was buried surrounded by people who loved him dearly.

In the five years since Henri's death a number of books, articles, anthologies and films have appeared which explore and celebrate his uniquely Christian teaching, and a Henri Nouwen society has formed. Henri's spirit seems to impact and inspire more and more people all the time.

This book attempts to fill a gap in Henri's many writings. Although Jesus was the underlying concern of most of his books, he never wrote a book about the life of Jesus. It was Robert Ellsberg of Orbis books who had the idea for a book about Jesus which would be gathered from Henri's remarks about Jesus in his other writings. It was my good fortune to be given the opportunity to make this idea a reality.

The version of the Bible cited is the New Jerusalem Bible, except where otherwise noted. Robert Ellsberg and I have chosen to illustrate this book with several drawings of the life of Christ by Rembrandt, who, as already noted, played a critical role in Henri's spiritual life.

I think you will enjoy this book more if I explain how it is set up. Each chapter is inspired by a scene from the gospels, and these chapters are arranged in order, beginning with The Annunciation and The Visitation. However, I put in several chapters at the beginning of the book which deal with important general concepts Henri Nouwen taught about God and Jesus. These chapters are called Spiritual Living, God's Hidden Way, Descending with Jesus, and God and the World. After these chapters, the Gospel story itself begins.

The chapters themselves also follow a pattern which I can explain in advance: each one begins with a biblical quotation, followed by reflections by Henri. Another, more general remark by Henri is set in the narrow outside column as a kind of epigraph. These three elements—the scriptural text, the reflections and the epigraph—are gathered around a theme which is sufficiently self-contained that you can read and meditate on it alone and read this book one chapter at a time if you like.

In what follows we have a chance to return to passages in the Gospel which we all know and remember, but to see them with new eyes. Henri will be with us on the journey, sharing with us his insights and telling us what these stories have meant to him. May the Spirit of Jesus be with us, too.

Michael O'Laughlin
Carlisle, Massachusetts, 2001

❧ God's Way ❧

Jesus is mocked. New York, the Pierpont Morgan Library/Art Resource, NY

Spiritual Living

Now, when I came to you, brothers, I did not come with any brilliance of oratory or wise argument to announce to you the mystery of God. I was resolved that the only knowledge I would have while I was with you was knowledge of Jesus, and of him as the crucified Christ. I came among you in weakness.

—1 Corinthians 2:1-3

Laying Open My Life

Even though following Jesus might be a more and more hidden journey for me, I do not think it should ever be a private journey. "Laying down your life for your friend" is what Jesus asks of me. For me that includes communicating as honestly as possible the pains and the joys, the darkness and the light, the fatigue and the vitality, the despair and the hope of going with Jesus to places where I would rather not go. By giving words to these intimate experiences I can make my own life available to others and thus become a witness to the word of life whom "I have heard, seen with my own eyes, watched and touched with my own hands" (1 John 1:1).[1]

This book is based upon the conviction that love is stronger than fear, though it may often seem that the opposite is true. "Perfect love casts out all fear," says St. John in the same letter. In this book I hope to search for signs of this perfect love and look for ways to follow those signs. I hope to show the possibility of a spiritual movement: the movement out of the house of fear into the house of love. But is it possible in the midst of this fear-provoking world to live in the house of love and listen there to the questions raised by the Lord of love? Or are we so

If you were to ask me point-blank: "What does it mean to you to live spiritually?" I would have to reply: "Living with Jesus at the center." There are always countless questions, problems, discussions and difficulties that demand one's attention. Despite this, when I look back over the last thirty years of my life, I can say that, for me, the person of Jesus has come to be more and more important. Specifically, this means that what matters increasingly is getting to know Jesus and living in solidarity with him. There was a time when I got so immersed in problems of Church and society that my whole life had become a sort of drawn-out, wearisome discussion. Jesus had been pushed into the background or had himself become just another problem. Fortunately, it hasn't stayed that way. Jesus has stepped out in front again, so to speak, and asked me: "And you, who do you say that I am?" It has become

clearer to me than ever that my personal relationship with Jesus is the heart of my existence. It is about Jesus, above all, that I want to write to you, and I want to do so in a personal way.[2]

accustomed to living in fear that we have become deaf to the voice that says: "Do not be afraid." This reassuring voice, which repeats over and over again: "Do not be afraid, have no fear," is the voice we most need to hear.[3]

Detail of
Jesus heals the blind man.

God's Hidden Way

Jesus said to them, "Have you never read in the scriptures:
The stone which the builders rejected has become the
cornerstone; this is the Lord's doing and we marvel at it."
—Matthew 21:42

Learning to See

The way of God is the way of weakness. The great news of the Gospel is precisely that God became small and vulnerable, and hence bore fruit among us. The most fruitful life ever lived is the life of Jesus, who did not cling to his divine power but became as we are (see Philippians 2:6-7). Jesus brought us new life in ultimate vulnerability. He came to us as a small child, dependent on the care and protection of others. He lived for us as a poor preacher, without any political, economic, or military power. He died for us nailed on a cross as a useless criminal. It is in this extreme vulnerability that our salvation was won. The fruit of this poor and failing existence is eternal life for all who believe in him. It is very hard for us to grasp even a little bit of the mystery of God's vulnerability. Yet, when we have eyes to see and ears to hear we can see it in many ways and in many places. We can see it when a child is born, the fruit of the love of two people who came together without defenses and embraced each other in weakness. We can see it in the graceful smiles of poor people and in the warm affection of the handicapped. We can see it every time people ask forgiveness and are reconciled.[5]

Hidden among Us

In our time with such an emphasis on visibility, the hidden life of Jesus is of special importance for a deeper understanding of our lives in the Spirit. The hidden life of

Now that Christianity has become one of the major world religions and millions of people utter the name of Jesus every day, it's hard for us to believe that Jesus revealed God in hiddenness. But neither Jesus' life nor his death nor his resurrection were intended to astound us with the great power of God. God became a lowly, hidden, almost invisible God.[4]

Jesus reveals to us the hidden presence of God. God who is the most different one, the most distinct one, the most "other," became the most hidden one, the one who is most the same. The experience of being the same, of being one with others, of being truly part of humanity, is a profoundly joyful and freeing experience. We are hidden in creation, hidden among our fellow human beings. That is the basis of true humility. We are to live close to the ground of our humanity. We are dust returning to dust. This humility is not self-rejecting, but self-affirming, since it offers a deeper sense of our embeddedness. Everything that Jesus says and does during his public life needs to be heard and seen as coming from the one whose life is first and foremost a life hidden among us. Jesus' death then becomes the full living out of this hiddenness. He lives his life out in such an intimate solidarity with us that we can say that he is more fully alive than any other human being. It is through this human "sameness" that we can come to share in his divine life.[6]

Descending with Jesus

You are well aware of the generosity which our Lord Jesus Christ had, that, although he was rich, he became poor for your sake, so that you should become rich through his poverty.   *—2 Corinthians 8:9*

The Path Chosen by Jesus

I want to write to you about the love of God become visible in Jesus. How is that love made visible through Jesus? It is made visible in the descending way. That is the great mystery of the Incarnation. God has descended to us human beings to become a human being with us; and once among us, descended to the total dereliction of one condemned to death. It isn't easy really to feel and understand from the inside this descending way of Jesus. Every fiber of our being rebels against it. We don't mind paying attention to poor people from time to time; but descending to a state of poverty and becoming poor with the poor, that we don't want to do. And yet that is the way Jesus chose as the way to know God.

In the first century of Christianity there was already a hymn being sung about this descending way of Jesus. Paul puts it into his Letter to the Philippians in order to commend to his people the descending direction on the ladder of life. He writes:

> Make your own the mind of Christ Jesus:
> Who, being in the form of God,
> did not count equality with God
> something to be grasped.
> But he emptied himself,
> taking the form of a slave,
> becoming as human beings are;
> and being in every way like a human being,

In the Gospel, it's quite obvious that Jesus chose the descending way. He chose it not once but over and over again. At each critical moment he deliberately sought the way downwards.[7]

he was humbler yet,
even to accepting death, death on a cross.

Here, expressed in summary but very plain terms, is the way of God's love. It is a way that goes down further and further into the greatest destitution: the destitution of a criminal whose life is taken from him. You may wonder, at this point, whether Jesus isn't a masochist in search of misery. The opposite is true. The gospel of Jesus is a gospel of peace and joy, not of self-disdain and self-torment. The descending way of Jesus is the way to a new fellowship in which we human beings can reach new life and celebrate it happily together.

How is it possible for the descending way of Jesus to give rise to a new kind of community, grounded in love? It's very important that you come to understand this from the inside, so that a desire to follow Jesus in his descending way can gradually grow in you.[8]

Descending in Unity

Everything in me wants to move upward. Downward mobility with Jesus goes radically against my inclinations, against the advice of the world surrounding me, and against the culture of which I am a part. In choosing to become poor with the poor at L'Arche, I still hope to gain praise for that choice. Wherever I turn I am confronted with my deep-seated resistance against following Jesus on his way to the cross and my countless ways of avoiding poverty, whether material, intellectual, or emotional. Only Jesus, in whom the fullness of God dwells, could freely and fully choose to be completely poor.

I see clearer now that choosing to become poor is choosing to make every part of my journey with Jesus. Becoming truly poor is impossible, but "nothing is impossible to God" (Luke 1:37). In and through Jesus I believe that the way to true poverty will open itself to me. After all, it is not my poverty that has any value, but only God's poverty, which becomes visible through my life.

This sounds unreal, but when I saw the men and women who announced their covenant with Jesus and the poor, I saw how real this downward way of Jesus is and how, if I go this way, I go not alone, but as a member of the "body of Jesus." Seldom have I experienced so directly the difference between individual heroism and communal obedience. Whenever I think about becoming poor as something I must accomplish, I become depressed. But as soon as I realize that my brothers and sisters call me to go this way with them in obedience to Jesus, I am filled with hope and joy.[9]

Detail of *Jesus is mocked.*

God and the World

The world lies in the power of the Evil One. Indeed, the powers of darkness rule the world. We should not be surprised when we see human suffering and pain all around us. But we should be surprised by joy every time we see that God, not the Evil One, has the last word. By entering into the world and confronting the Evil One with the fullness of Divine Goodness, the way was opened for us to live in the world, no longer as victims, but as free men and women, guided, not by optimism, but by hope.[10]

For this is how God loved the world: he gave his only Son, so that everyone who believes in him may not perish but may have eternal life. —*John 3:16*

Becoming Part of God's Love

Jesus sees the evil in this world as a lack of trust in God's love. He makes us see that we persistently fall back on ourselves, rely more on ourselves than on God, and are inclined more to love of self than to love of God. So we remain in the darkness. If we walk in the light, then we are enabled to acknowledge in joy and gratitude that everything good, beautiful and true comes from God and is offered to us in love.

Jesus shows us that true love, the love that comes from God, makes no distinction between friends and foes, between people who are for us and people who are against us, people who do us a favor and people who do us ill. God makes no such distinction. He loves all human beings, good or bad, with the same unconditional love. This all-embracing love Jesus offers to us, and he invites us to make this love visible in our lives.

If our love, like God's love, embraces foe as well as friend, we have become children of God and are no longer children of suspicion, jealousy, violence, war and death. Our love for our enemies shows to whom we really belong. It shows our true home. Jesus states it so clearly: "Love your enemies and do good to them, and lend without any hope of return. You will have a great reward, and you will be children of the Most High, for he himself is kind to the ungrateful and the wicked."

There you have it: the love of God is an unconditional love, and only that love can empower us to live together without violence. When we know that God loves us deeply and will always go on loving us, whoever we are and whatever we do, it becomes possible to expect no more of our fellow men and women than they are able to give, to forgive them generously when they have offended us, and always to respond to their hostility with love. By doing so we make visible a new way of being human and a new way of responding to our world problems.

Mrs. Aquino realized that hatred for President Marcos could not lead to peace in the Philippines. Martin Luther King understood that hating whites could not lead to true equality among Americans. Gandhi knew that hating the British could not bring about genuine independence in India. A new world without slaughter and massacre can never be the fruit of hatred. It is the fruit of the love of "your Father in heaven, for he causes his sun to rise on the bad as well as the good, and sends down rain to fall on the upright and the wicked alike." It is the fruit of God's love which we limited humans are to make visible in our lives in accordance with the words of Jesus: "You must therefore set no bounds to your love, just as your heavenly Father sets none to his."

Whenever, contrary to the world's vindictiveness, we love our enemy, we exhibit something of the perfect love of God, whose will is to bring all human beings together as children of one Father. Whenever we forgive instead of letting fly at one another, bless instead of cursing one another, tend one another's wounds instead of rubbing salt into them, hearten instead of discouraging one another, give hope instead of driving one another to despair, hug instead of harassing one another, welcome instead of cold-shouldering one another, thank instead of criticizing one another, praise instead of maligning one another . . . in short, whenever we opt for and not against one another, we make God's unconditional love visible; we are diminishing violence and giving birth to a new community.[11]

The world is only evil when you become its slave.[12]

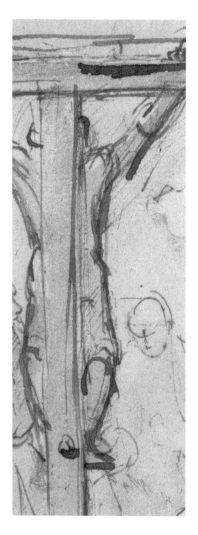

Detail of *Jesus is given vinegar to drink on the cross.*

✴ The Gospel Begins ✴

The Annunciation.
Besançon, Musée des Beaux-Arts/Art Resource, NY

The Annunciation

In the sixth month the angel Gabriel was sent by God to a town in Galilee called Nazareth, to a virgin betrothed to a man named Joseph, of the House of David, and the virgin's name was Mary. He went in and said to her, "Rejoice, you who enjoy God's favor! The Lord is with you."

—Luke 1:26-8

Mary's full affirmation of God's election made her the Mother of God.[1]

Saying Yes to God

My prayer life has been quite difficult lately. During my morning meditation I think about a thousand things except God and God's presence in my life. I am worrying, brooding, and agonizing, but not really praying.

To my own surprise the only prayer that offers me some peace and consolation is the prayer to Mary. My meditation on the Annunciation brought me real peace and joy, while reflections on other mysteries could not keep me focused. As I tried to simply be with Mary and listen to her words, "You see before you the Lord's servant; let it happen to me as you have said" (Luke 1:38), I discovered a restful peace. Instead of thinking about these words and trying to understand them, I just listened to them being spoken for me.

Mary is so open, so free, so trusting. She is completely willing to hear words that go far beyond her own comprehension. She knows that the words spoken to her by the angel come from God. She seeks clarification, but she does not question their authority. She senses that the message of Gabriel will radically interrupt her life, and she is afraid, but she does not withdraw. When she hears the words "You will bear a son . . . he will be called the son of the Most High," she asks, "But how can this come about, since I have no knowledge of man?" Then she hears what no other human being ever heard: "The Holy Spirit will come upon you and the power of the Most High will cover you with its shadow." She responded with a complete surrender and thus became not only the mother of Jesus but also the mother of all who believe in him. ". . . let it happen to me as you have said" (Luke 1:31, 34-35, 38).

I keep listening to these words as words that summarize the deepest possible response to God's loving action within us. God wants to let the Holy Spirit guide our lives, but are we prepared to let it happen? Just being with Mary and the angel and hearing their words—words which changed the course of history—bring me peace and rest.

I shared this experience with Père André this morning. He said, "Just stay there. Stay with Mary. Trust that she will show you the way. Do not move on as long as you find peace and rest with her. It is clear that she wants your attention. Give it to her, and you will soon understand why it is you are so distracted."

Simple, good, and consoling advice. I do not have to move faster than I can. I have received permission to stay in the place where I am consoled. It is the place where Mary says "Yes" to God's love.[2]

How Mary Protects Christianity

God chose to take flesh in the woman who had found favor in God's eyes and had responded to that favor with a full "yes." Her response was not only an initial agreement but a lifelong obedience to God's redemptive presence. In this obedience she followed Jesus in the most perfect way. Her life was a life of always fuller abandonment to the divine will, a total emptying out in faith, a full entering into the darkness of her Son's death. There is no other human being in whom we can see so fully what it means to receive the love of a God who loves us so much that he sent his own Son. She has known more blessing and more suffering than anyone else in all humanity. In her we see most fully what it means to be redeemed.

Thus Mary protects Christianity from becoming a system of ideas, doctrines, opinions, or convictions. She

Detail of *The Annunciation.*

constantly keeps before us that most intimate relationship with her Son. Her complete obedience, radical humility, and unwavering faithfulness show us what a life of following Jesus truly can be. Following Jesus does not mean clinging to an idea or holding on to a principle. It is walking the path of the one who gave his life for his friends and called his followers to do the same. Mary's whole being is in the service of Jesus. She is totally Mother, totally given to letting Jesus be born into this world, not only long ago in Bethlehem, but today and always in the heart of anyone who wants to find God. Her whole being is for Jesus. Seeing Mary always means seeing the Mother of God. Knowing Mary always means knowing the one who gives life to God.[3]

The Visitation

Your own growth cannot take place without growth in others. You are part of a body. When you change, the whole body changes. It is very important for you to remain deeply connected with the larger community to which you belong.[4]

As soon as Elizabeth heard Mary's greeting, the child leapt in her womb and Elizabeth was filled with the Holy Spirit. She gave a loud cry and said, "Of all women you are the most blessed, and blessed is the fruit of your womb."

—Luke 1:41-2

Mary Was Not Left Alone

In recent months the story of Mary's visit to her cousin Elizabeth has become very dear to me.

Mary receives the great and shocking news that she is going to become the Mother of the "son of the Most High." This news is so incomprehensible and so radically interrupts Mary's humble life that she finds herself totally alone. How can Joseph or any of her friends or relatives understand her situation? With whom can she share this most intimate knowledge, which remains inexplicable even to herself?

God offers Mary an intimate, human friend with whom she can share what seems incommunicable. Elizabeth, like Mary, has experienced divine intervention and has been called to a response of faith. She can be with Mary in a way no one else possibly could.

Thus, it is understandable that "Mary set out at that time and went as quickly as she could into the hill country to a town in Judah" (Luke 1:39) to visit Elizabeth.

I am deeply moved by this simple and mysterious encounter. In the midst of an unbelieving, doubting, pragmatic, and cynical world, two women meet each other and affirm in each other the promise given to them. The humanly impossible has happened to them. God has come to them to begin the salvation promised through the ages. Through these two women God has decided to change the course of history. Who could ever understand? Who could ever believe it? Who could ever let it happen? But Mary says, "Let it happen to me," and she immediately realizes that only Elizabeth will be able to affirm her "yes." For three months Mary and Elizabeth live together and encourage each other to truly accept the motherhood given to them. Mary's presence makes Elizabeth more fully aware of becoming the mother of the "prophet of the Most High" (Luke 1:76), and Elizabeth's presence allows Mary to grow in the knowledge of becoming the mother of the "son of the Most High" (Luke 1:32).

Neither Mary nor Elizabeth had to wait in isolation. They could wait together and thus deepen in each other their faith in God, for whom nothing is impossible. Thus, God's most radical intervention into history was listened to and received in community.

The story of the Visitation teaches me the meaning of friendship and community. How can I ever let God's grace fully work in my life unless I live in a community of people who can affirm it, deepen it, and strengthen it? We cannot live this new life alone. God does not want to isolate us by his grace. On the contrary, he wants us to form new friendships and a new community—holy places where his grace can grow to fullness and bear fruit.

So often new life appears in the Church because of an encounter. Dorothy Day never claimed The Catholic Worker as her own invention. She always spoke of it as the fruit of her encounter with Peter Maurin. Jean Vanier never claims that he started L'Arche on his own. He always points to his encounter with Père Thomas Philippe as the true beginning of L'Arche. In such encounters two or more people are able to affirm each other in their gifts and encourage each other to "let it happen to them." In this way, new hope is given to the world.

"Yes, blessed is she who believed that the promise made her by the Lord would be fulfilled."—Luke 1:45

Elizabeth helped Mary to become the Mother of God. Mary helped Elizabeth to become the mother of her Son's prophet, John the Baptist. God may choose us individually, but he always wants us to come together to allow his choice to come to maturity.[5]

Childhood

Jesus came to reunite, to heal, to form bonds, to reconcile.[6]

Now in Jerusalem there was a man named Simeon. He was an upright and devout man; he looked forward to the restoration of Israel and the Holy Spirit rested on him. It had been revealed to him by the Holy Spirit that he would not see death until he had set eyes on the Christ of the Lord. Prompted by the Spirit he came to the Temple, and when the parents brought in the child Jesus to do for him what the Law required, he took him into his arms and blessed God, and he said:

> *Now, Master, you are letting*
> *your servant go in peace as you promised,*
> *for my eyes have seen the salvation*
> *which you have made ready in the sight of the*
>   *nations,*
> *a light of revelation for the gentiles*
> *and glory for your people Israel.*

> *—Luke 2:25-32*

Why God Came to Us as a Baby

God says, "I love you with an everlasting love," and Jesus came to tell us that. We are the Beloved, not because we did anything, not because we proved ourselves. Basically, God loves us whatever we do. If that's true, these few years that we are in the world, we are sent to say, in the midst of our life, "Yes, God, I love you, too."

Just as God cares for us, it's very important that we care for God in the world. If God is born like a little baby, God cannot walk or speak unless someone teaches God. That's the story of Jesus, who needs human beings in order to grow. God is saying, "I want to be weak so you can love me. What better way to help you respond to my love than becoming weak so you can care for me?" God becomes a stumbling God who falls at the cross, who dies for us, and

Presentation at the Temple.
Paris, Louvre/Art Resource, NY

who is totally in need of love. God does this so that we can get close. The God who loves us is a God who becomes vulnerable, dependent in the manger and dependent on the cross, a God who basically is saying, "Are you there for me?"[7]

Jesus Embraces Not Only Vulnerability, but Obscurity, too

The greatest part of Jesus' life is a hidden life. It is a life lived under the authority of his parents during which he grew to maturity and increased in wisdom, in stature, and in favor with God and people (Luke 2:39-40; 51-2). Although the gospels remain silent about this period of Jesus' life, this silence is very revealing. It reveals that the good news is first of all that God came to live among us, to be Emmanuel, God with us, and to share the ordinariness of our daily existence. Jesus wanted to be known as we are known.[8]

> In God's eyes the most significant is
> often the most hidden.[9]

Baptism and Temptation

Then Jesus appeared; he came from Galilee to the Jordan to be baptized by John. —Matthew 3:13

Humility before John

Jesus, who is without sin, stands in line with sinners waiting to be baptized by John. As Jesus starts his ministry, he chooses to enter into solidarity with sinful humanity. "John tried to dissuade him with the words, 'It is I who need baptism from you, and yet you come to me.' But Jesus replied, 'Leave it like this for the time being; it is fitting that we should, in this way, do all that righteousness demands'" (Matthew 3:14-15).

Here we see how Jesus clearly chooses the way of humility. He does not appear with great fanfare as a powerful savior, announcing a new order. On the contrary, he comes quietly, with the many sinners who are receiving a baptism of repentance. His choice is affirmed by the voice from heaven: "This is my Son, the Beloved; my favor rests on him" (Matthew 3:17).

It is hard to believe that God would reveal his divine presence in the self-emptying, humble way of the man from Nazareth. So much in me seeks influence, power, success and popularity. But the way of Jesus is the way of hiddenness, powerlessness, and littleness.[11]

Affirmation as the Beloved

I very much believe that the core moment of Jesus' public life was the baptism in the Jordan, when Jesus heard the affirmation, "You are my beloved on whom my favor rests." That is the core experience of Jesus. He is reminded in a deep, deep way of who he is. The temptations in the desert are temptations to move him away from that spiritual

Becoming the beloved means letting the truth of our belovedness become enfleshed in everything we think, say, or do. It entails a long and painful process of appropriation or, better, incarnation.[10]

identity. He was tempted to believe he was someone else: You are the one who can turn stone into bread. You are the one who can jump from the temple. You are the one who can make others bow to your power. Jesus said, "No, no, no. I am the Beloved from God." I think his whole life is continually claiming that identity in the midst of everything. There are times in which he is praised, times when he is despised or rejected, but he keeps saying, "Others will leave me alone, but my Father will not leave me alone. I am the beloved Son of God. I am the hope found in that identity."[12]

Detail of
Presentation at the Temple.

And at once the Spirit drove him into the desert and he remained there for forty days, and was put to the test by Satan. He was with the wild animals, and the angels looked after him.
—Mark 1:12-3

❋ Reaching Out ❋

Jesus in the house of Martha and Mary.
Haarlem, Teylers Museum

Jesus' Preaching in Nazareth

Jesus, with the power of the Spirit in him, returned to Galilee; and his reputation spread throughout the countryside. He taught in their synagogues and everyone glorified him. He came to Nazareth, where he had been brought up, and went into the synagogue on the Sabbath day as he usually did. He stood up to read, and they handed him the scroll of the prophet Isaiah . . .

—Luke 4:14-7

Waiting to Hear Jesus

You are looking for ways to meet Jesus. You are trying to meet him not only in your mind but also in your body. You seek his affection, and you know that this affection involves his body as well as yours. He became flesh for you so that you could encounter him in the flesh and receive his love in the flesh.

But something remains in you that prevents this meeting. There is still a lot of shame and guilt stuck away in your body, blocking the presence of Jesus. You do not fully feel at home in your body; you look down on it as if it were not a good enough, beautiful enough, or pure enough place to meet Jesus.

When you look attentively at your life, you will see how filled it has been with fears, especially fears of people in authority: your parents, your teachers, your bishops, your spiritual guides, even your friends. You never felt equal to them and kept putting yourself down in front of them. For most of your life, you have felt as if you needed their permission to be yourself.

Think about Jesus. He was totally free before the authorities of his time. He told people not to be guided by the behavior of the scribes and Pharisees. Jesus came among us as an equal, a brother. He broke down the

Jesus was truly free. His freedom was rooted in his spiritual awareness that he was the Beloved Child of God. He knew in the depth of his being that he belonged to God before he was born, that he was sent into the world to proclaim God's love, and that he would return to God after his mission was fulfilled. This knowledge gave him the freedom to speak and act without having to please the world and the power to respond to people's pain with the healing love of God.[1]

pyramidal structures of relationship between God and people as well as those among people and offered a new model: the circle, where God lives in full solidarity with the people and the people with one another.

You will not be able to meet Jesus in your body while your body remains full of doubts and fears. Jesus came to free you from these bonds and to create in you a space where you can be with him. He wants you to live the freedom of the children of God.[2]

Letting God's Word Transform Us as We Listen

Often we think about the word as an exhortation to go out and change our lives. But the full power of the word lies, not in how we apply it to our lives after we have heard it, but in its transforming power that does its divine work as we listen.

The Gospels are filled with examples of God's presence in the word. Personally, I am always touched by the story of Jesus in the synagogue of Nazareth. There he read from Isaiah:

> The Spirit of the Lord is on me,
>   for he has anointed me
>   to bring good news to the afflicted.
>   He has sent me to proclaim liberty to captives,
>   sight to the blind,
>   to let the oppressed go free,
>   to proclaim a year of favor from the Lord.
>
> Luke 4:18-9

After having read these words, Jesus said, "This text is being fulfilled today even while you are listening." Suddenly, it becomes clear that the afflicted, the captives, the blind, and the oppressed are not people somewhere outside of the synagogue who, someday, will be liberated; they are the people who are listening. And it is in the listening that God becomes present and heals.

The Word of God is not a word to apply in our daily lives at some later date; it is a word to heal us through, and in, our listening here and now.

The questions therefore are: How does God come to me as I listen to the word? Where do I discern the healing hand of God touching me through the word? How are my sadness, my grief, and my mourning being transformed at this very moment? Do I sense the fire of God's love purifying my heart and giving me new life? These questions lead me to the sacrament of the word, the sacred place of God's real presence.

At first this might sound quite new for a person living in a society in which the main value of the word is its applicability. But most of us know already, generally unconsciously, of the healing and destroying power of the spoken word. When someone says to me, "I love you," or "I hate you," I am not just receiving some useful information. These words do something in me. They make my blood move, my heart beat, my breathing speed up. They make me feel and think differently. They lift me up to a new way of being and give me another knowledge of myself. These words have the power to heal or to destroy me.[3]

They said, "This is Joseph's son, surely?" But he replied, "No doubt you will quote me the saying, 'Physician, heal yourself,' and tell me, 'We have heard all that happened in Capernaum, do the same here in your own country.'" And he went on, "In truth I tell you, no prophet is ever accepted in his own country."
—Luke 4:22-4

They sprang to their feet and hustled him out of the town and they took him up to the brow of the hill their town was built on, intending to throw him off the cliff, but he passed straight through the crowd and walked away.
—Luke 4:29-30

The Family of Jesus

The mission is always first of all to our own, our family, our friends, those who are an intimate part of our lives. That is not a very comfortable realization. I always find it harder to speak about Jesus to those who know me intimately than to those who have never had to deal with my "peculiar ways of being." Still there lies a great challenge here. Somehow the authenticity of our experience is tested by our parents, our spouses, our children, our brothers and sisters, all those who know us all too well.[4]

He went home again, and once more such a crowd collected that they could not even have a meal. When his relations heard of this, they set out to take charge of him; they said, "He is out of his mind." —Mark 3:20-1

Jesus Distanced Himself from His Family

Today is the Feast of St. Joseph, the righteous man. Often the family of Jesus is portrayed as the model for all families. But a closer look at the way Joseph, Mary and Jesus lived together evokes little desire for imitation. Indeed, Joseph was a very decent man. He didn't want to give his pregnant girlfriend a bad reputation, and after a reassuring dream, he married her. But was it a happy life? When Jesus was twelve they lost him in the crowd, and when they found him, after three days of anxiously looking, their question: "Why did you do this to us?" was answered by something close to a reproach: "Did you not know that I must be in my Father's house?" (Luke 2:49). This response, "But didn't you know I have more important things to do than pay attention to you," is hardly consoling.

All the other references to Jesus' family life are more disturbing than consoling. At Cana when Mary asks for his help, Jesus says, "What do you want from me? My hour has not come yet" (John 2:4). When, later, Jesus receives a message saying, "Look, your mother and brothers and sisters are outside asking for you," he replies, "Who are my mother and my brothers?" (Mark 3:32-33). Finally we find Mary standing under the cross. Seeing his mother and his beloved disciple, John, Jesus says to his mother, "Woman, this is your son" (John 19:26). About Joseph there is no word. What happened to him? Did he die?

In this time of broken families, of separation and divorce, of children with only one parent, and of mothers and fathers in great anxiety about their suicidal or drug-using kids, the seemingly quite dysfunctional family of Jesus may offer us some solace! It is clear to me that Jesus is quite ambivalent if not negative about so-called family values such as family harmony, filial affection, staying together at all costs. I wonder if our church's elevation of celibacy, especially for those who want to serve God, does not have its roots in the quite disturbing situation of Jesus' own family.

But Joseph is a saint! He lived it all in a great hidden-ness. Ignored by the Gospel writers, and by the early church, he emerges today as a man trusting in God even when there was hardly anything for him to hold on to.[5]

Family and Individuation

When Jesus came to his hometown and began to teach the people in the synagogue, they said: "Isn't this the car-penter's son? Is not his mother called Mary? And are not his brothers James and Joseph and Simon and Judas? And are not all his sisters with us? Where then did this man get all this? And they took offense at him" (Matthew 13:54-7). It fascinates me that Jesus finally had to establish his author-ity outside the circle of his family, taking distance from them: in the temple when he was twelve years old, in Cana when Mary wanted to intervene, during his preaching or when the family wanted to visit him.

Family is where we grow up into adult, mature people, but we have to leave our families to fulfill our deepest voca-tion. Family can give us a sense of belonging, but in order to claim our deepest belonging, our belonging to God, we have to move away from those who pretend to know us and discover the deepest source of our lives. Our parents, brothers, and sisters do not own us. Without leaving them it is hard to fully become free and listen to the One who called us even before we were born.

Jesus often had to say no to his family in order to be able to say a full yes to his Father in heaven.[6]

He replied, "Who are my mother and my brothers?" And looking at those sitting in a circle round him, he said, "Here are my mother and my brothers. And any-one who does the will of God, that person is my brother and sister and mother."—Mark 3:33-5

Conversation with Nicodemus

➤

If anyone had asked me in the past, "Who is the center of your life?" I would have answered without much hesitation, "Jesus, who called me to follow him." But now I do not dare say that so easily. The struggle to become a full member of a community of faith has proved to be a struggle to let go of many idols along the way and to choose again and again to follow Jesus and him alone.[7]

There was one of the Pharisees called Nicodemus, a leader of the Jews, who came to Jesus by night and said, "Rabbi, we know that you have come from God as a teacher, for no one could perform the signs that you do unless God were with him." Jesus answered: "In all truth I tell you, no one can see the kingdom of God without being born from above." Nicodemus said, "How can anyone who is already old be born? Is it possible to go back into the womb again and be born?" Jesus replied, "In all truth I tell you, no one can enter the kingdom of God without being born through water and the Spirit; what is born of human nature is human; what is born of the Spirit is spirit. Do not be surprised when I say: you must be born from above."

—*John 3:1-7*

Valuing One's Dignity and One's Attachments over Jesus

Jesus not only had good, faithful friends willing to follow him wherever he went and fierce enemies who couldn't wait to get rid of him, but also many sympathizers who were attracted, but afraid at the same time.

The rich young man loved Jesus but couldn't give up his wealth to follow him. Nicodemus admired Jesus but was afraid to lose the respect of his own colleagues. I am becoming more and more aware of the importance of looking at these fearful sympathizers because that is the group I find myself mostly gravitating toward.

I love Jesus but want to hold on to my own friends even when they do not lead me closer to Jesus. I love Jesus but want to hold on to my own independence even when that independence brings me no real freedom. I love Jesus but do not want to lose the respect of my professional colleagues, even though I know that their respect does not make me grow spiritually. I love Jesus but do not want to give up my writing plans, travel plans, and speaking plans, even when these plans are often more to my glory than to the glory of God.

So I am like Nicodemus, who came by night, said safe things about Jesus to his colleagues, and expressed his guilt by bringing to the grave more myrrh and aloes than needed or desired.

To his colleagues, the Pharisees, Nicodemus said, "our Law does not allow us to pass judgment on anyone without first giving him a hearing and discovering what he is doing" (John 7:51). These are careful words. They are spoken to people who hate Jesus. But they are spoken on their terms. They say, "Even if you hate Jesus and desire to kill him, do not lose your dignity, follow your own rules." Nicodemus said it to save Jesus, but he didn't want to lose his friends. It didn't work. He was ridiculed by his friends: "Are you a Galilean too? Go into the matter, and see for yourself: prophets do not arise from Galilee!" His personal and professional identity are attacked.

It is such a familiar scene. I have spoken like Nicodemus in episcopal committees and faculty meetings many times. Instead of speaking directly about my love for Jesus, I make a smart remark suggesting that maybe my friends should look at another side of the question. They usually respond by saying I have not studied my sources well enough, or that I seem to have some sentimental attachment that got in the way of a truly professional approach. Those who have said these things have had the power of right thinking and thus forced me to silence. But it has been fear that has prevented me from speaking from the heart and risking rejection.

Nicodemus deserves all my attention. Can I stay a Pharisee and follow Jesus too? Doesn't that condemn me to bringing costly spices to the grave when it is too late?[8]

Detail of *Jesus' disappearance in Emmaus.*

A Call to Friendship

Dear Lord, you said to your disciples: "All I have learned from my Father, I have made known to you." That is the intimacy to which you invite those who believe in you. You do not want to hide anything from us. You want to give us all you have, all you are.[9]

The next day as John stood there again with two of his disciples, Jesus went past, and John looked towards him and said, "Look, there is the lamb of God." And the two disciples heard what he said and followed Jesus. Jesus turned round, saw them following and said, "What do you want?" They answered, "Rabbi"—which means teacher—"where do you live?" He replied, "Come and see."

—John 1:35-9

Dwelling with Jesus

As I read the Gospels I am struck how often images connected with a new dwelling place are used. John the Evangelist describes Jesus as the Word of God who came into the world and pitched his tent among us (John 1:14). He also tells us how the first disciples asked Jesus when they first met him, "Teacher, where do you live?" and were invited to stay in his home (John 1:38-9). Here we are already made aware that following Jesus means changing places, entering into a new milieu, and living in new company. The full meaning of this gradually unfolds in the Gospels. We come to see that Jesus not only invites his followers to live with him in the same house, but that he himself is the house.[10]

Entering the House of Love

Intimacy is beyond fear. Those who have experienced the intimacy to which Jesus invites us know that they no longer need to worry about getting too close or becoming too distant. When Jesus says: "It is I; do not be afraid," he reveals a new space in which we can move freely without fear. This intimate space is not a fine line between distance and closeness, but a wide field of movement in which the question of whether we are close or distant is no longer the guiding question.

When St. John says that fear is driven out by perfect love, he points to a love that comes from God, a divine love. He does not speak about human affection, psychological compatibility, mutual attraction, or deep interpersonal feelings. All of that has its value and beauty, but the perfect love about which St. John speaks embraces and transcends all feelings, emotions, and passions. The perfect love that drives out all fear is the divine love in which we are invited to participate. The home, the intimate place, the place of true belonging, is therefore not a place made by human hands. It is fashioned for us by God, who came to pitch his tent among us, invite us to his place, and prepare a room for us in his own house.

Words for "home" are often used in the Old and New Testaments. The Psalms are filled with a yearning to dwell in the house of God, to take refuge under God's wings, and to find protection in God's holy temple; they praise God's holy place, God's wonderful tent, God's firm refuge. We might even say that "to dwell in God's house" summarizes all the aspirations expressed in these inspired prayers. It is therefore highly significant that St. John describes Jesus as the Word of God pitching his tent among us (John 1:14). He not only tells us that Jesus invites him and his brother Andrew to stay in his home (John 1:38-39), but he also shows how Jesus gradually reveals that he himself is the new temple (John 2:19) and the new refuge (Matthew 11:28). This is most fully expressed in the farewell address, where Jesus reveals himself as the new home: "Make your home in me, as I make mine in you" (John 15:4).

Jesus, in whom the fullness of God dwells, has become our home. By making his home in us he allows us to make our home in him. By entering into the intimacy of our innermost self he offers us the opportunity to enter into his own intimacy with God. By choosing us as his preferred dwelling place he invites us to choose him as our preferred dwelling place. This is the mystery of the Incarnation.[11]

"You are my friends, if you do what I command you. I shall no longer call you servants, because a servant does not know the master's business. I call you friends . . . "
—John 15:14-5

His Ministry and Ours

⇻

We serve the world by being spiritually well. The first question is not, "How much do we do?" or "How many people do we help out?" but "Are we interiorly at peace?" The distinction between contemplation and action can be misleading. Jesus' actions flowed from his interior communion with God. His presence was healing, and it changed the world. In a sense he didn't do anything! "Everyone who touched him was healed."[12]

He then came down with them and stopped at a piece of level ground where there was a large gathering of his disciples, with a great crowd of people from all parts of Judaea and Jerusalem and the coastal region of Tyre and Sidon who had come to hear him and to be cured of their diseases. People tormented by unclean spirits were also cured, and everyone in the crowd was trying to touch him because power came out of him that cured them all.

—Luke 6:17-9

Being Rather than Doing

In the text in Luke we see that Jesus starts community right away. He does his whole ministry with others. He sent the disciples out to heal, drive out demons, and announce his coming. From the very beginning Jesus sees his task as a ministry with others. He goes out to minister with his disciples.

The Bible says that Jesus went out and the crowds were there. So he was one with God, then together with a few people, and then the crowds came. One of the things I like to say is that if you are living in communion with God and in community with people you cannot do other than minister. Ministry is not something you do next. I have a terribly hard time with ministry as something that consists of techniques you have to apply. Ministry is the overflow of your love for God and for your fellow human beings. Someone said to me, "Ministry is when two people toast their glasses of wine and something splashes over." Ministry is the extra. The question is not, "How do I bring all of these people to Jesus, or how do I make these people believe, or how do I now do the hard work of ministry?"

Ministry happens. I have done nothing here while on sabbatical to do ministry. I didn't come here to get people

Jesus heals the blind man.
Rotterdam, Museum Boymans-van
Beuningen/Art Resource, NY

who mostly don't go to church to join me in prayer and the Eucharist. I just started to pray, and invited one person to join me, and these others—neighbors and friends—simply came. I'm not concerned with fixing the marriage of the one who is considering divorce or convincing the woman who doesn't believe in Jesus. I'm here to say this is who I am, and to be there for others.

Jesus never did much ministry. Jesus spoke what his heart was full of. And anybody who touched him was healed. He didn't sit people down and diagnose them, or say to them, "I can help *you* but I can't help *you*." People touched him and were healed. He was even wondering what was happening. You cannot but minister if you are in communion with God and in communion with other people. People want to know where your energy comes from. They get the overflow. It's not something that requires professional credentials. Ministry isn't something you do for certain hours during the day and then you come home and relax. Who knows? Ministry might happen while you are relaxing.

Two words I think are helpful for ministry are "compassion" and "gratitude." Ministry happens when you participate in the mystery of being with. The whole incarnation, God-with-us, Emmanuel, is first of all being with people. Caring means "to cry out with." Compassion literally means "to be with those who suffer." Ministry means that we lift the incarnation—we lift the God who says, "I will be with you." We are to be precisely where people are vulnerable, not to fix it or to change it. That is an unintended fruit of it, but that is not why you are there. Compassion is the priesthood of Jesus—read the Letter to the Hebrews. Since nothing human was alien to him, he was the compassionate high priest. Jesus is first of all God-with-us. For thirty years he was just living in a small village, living the same life that we live. It was only for three years that he was preaching. So even when you look at it in a spiritual way, Jesus' ministry wasn't just the three years he was preaching. The mystery is that he shared our lives. God is a God-with-us. Ministry is being with the sick, the dying, being with people wherever they are, whatever their problems. We dare to be with them in their weakness and trust that if we are entering into people's vulnerable places, we will experience immense joy. That is the mystery of ministry.

You can't solve the world's problems, but you can be with people. I've been with two people who were dying in the last months. It wasn't a burden—it was a great joy to have the privilege to be there when they made their passage.[13]

A Sermon on a Mountainside

He went round the whole of Galilee teaching in their synagogues, proclaiming the good news of the kingdom and curing all kinds of disease and illness among the people. His fame spread throughout Syria, and those who were suffering from diseases and painful complaints of one kind and another, the possessed, epileptics, the paralyzed, were all brought to him, and he cured them. Large crowds followed him, coming from Galilee, the Decapolis, Jerusalem, Judaea, and Transjordan. Seeing the crowds, he went onto the mountain, and when he was seated his disciples came to him. Then he began to speak. —Matthew 4:23-5:2

God wants all of our heart, all of our mind, and all of our soul. It is this unconditional and unreserved love for God that leads to the care for our neighbor . . .[14]

The Sermon on the Mount Is Not about Morality, It Is about Jesus

The more you listen to God speaking within you, the sooner you will hear that voice inviting you to follow the way of Jesus. For Jesus' way is God's way and God's way is not for Jesus only but for everyone who is truly seeking God. Here we come up against the hard truth that the descending way of Jesus is also the way for us to find God. Jesus doesn't hesitate for a moment to make that clear. Soon after he has ended his period of fasting in the wilderness and called his first disciples to follow him, he says:

> How blessed are the poor in spirit . . .
> Blessed are the gentle . . .
> Blessed are those who mourn . . .
> Blessed are those who hunger and thirst for
>   uprightness
> Blessed are the merciful . . .
> Blessed are the pure in heart . . .
> Blessed are the peacemakers . . .

Blessed are those who are persecuted in the cause
of uprightness . . .

Jesus is drawing a self-portrait here and inviting his disciples to become like him. He will continue to speak in this way to the very end. Jesus never makes a distinction between himself and his followers. His sorrow will be theirs; his joy they too will taste. He says: "If they persecuted me, they will persecute you too; if they kept my word, they will keep yours as well." As he speaks, they too must speak; as he behaves, they too must behave; as he suffers, they too must suffer. In all things, Jesus is their example and even more than that. He is their model.[15]

Blessed Are the Poor

One member of our community has a limited vocabulary, but the words he knows best are "open heart." Whenever he prays for others he says: "I pray that you have an open heart." Those who hear his prayer are always deeply touched because it summarizes all we can ask for.

God's blessing is hidden in our littleness like a diamond in its setting. That is why Jesus said "Blessed are the poor" and "Blessed are those who mourn." Precisely where we cannot help ourselves, where we are poor and cry, the gifts of love, joy, peace and simple trust are held. Jesus did not say "Blessed are those who care for the poor," or "Blessed are those who console the mourners," because caring and consoling often happen from a place of strength, whereas God's love is revealed to us by Jesus coming among us in weakness, so too are God's blessings given to us through whom the world considers little, poor, weak, useless or marginal.[16]

The Heart of the Sermon Seems Impossibly Hard

Jesus said: *"Love your enemies, do good to those who hate you, bless those who curse you, pray for those who treat you badly. To anyone who slaps you on one cheek, present the other cheek as well; to anyone who takes your cloak from you, do not refuse your tunic. Give to everyone who asks you, and do not ask for your property back from someone who takes it. Treat others as you would like people to treat you . . . love your enemies and do good to them, and lend without any hope of return."*

These sayings express not only the essence of nonviolent resistance, but also the heart of Jesus' preaching. If anyone should ask you what are the most radical words in the gospel, you need not hesitate to reply: "Love your enemies." It's these words that reveal to us most clearly the kind of love proclaimed by Jesus. In these words we have the clearest expression of what it means to be a disciple of Jesus. Love for one's enemy is the touchstone of being a Christian.[17]

Turning the other cheek means showing our enemies that they can only be our enemies while supposing that we are anxiously clinging to our private property, whatever it is: our knowledge, our good name, our land, our money, or the many objects we have collected around us. But who will be our robber when everything he wants to steal from us becomes our gift to him? Once we have become poor, we can be a good host. It is indeed the paradox of hospitality that poverty makes a good host. Poverty is the inner disposition that allows us to take away our defenses and convert our enemies into friends. We can only perceive the stranger as an enemy as long as we have something to defend. But when we say, "Please enter—my house is your house, my joy is your joy, my sadness is your sadness and my life is your life," we have nothing to defend, since we have nothing to lose but all to give.[18]

"Do not judge, and you will not be judged; because the judgments you give are the judgments you will get. . ."
—Matthew 7:1-2

On Judging

Imagine your having no need at all to judge anybody. Imagine your having no desire to decide whether someone is a good or bad person. Imagine your being completely free from the feeling that you have to make up your mind about the morality of someone's behavior. Imagine that you could say: "I am judging no one!"

Imagine—Wouldn't that be true inner freedom? The desert fathers from the fourth century said: "Judging others is a heavy burden." I have had a few moments in my life during which I felt free from all judgments about others. It felt as if a heavy burden had been taken away from me. At those moments I experienced an immense love for everyone I met, heard about, or read about. A deep solidarity with all people and a deep desire to love them broke down all my inner walls and made my heart as wide as the universe.

One such moment occurred after a seven-month stay in a Trappist monastery. I was so full of God's goodness that I saw that goodness wherever I went, even behind the facades of violence, destruction, and crime. I had to restrain myself from embracing the women and men who sold me groceries, flowers, and a new suit. They all seemed like saints to me!

We all have these moments if we are attentive to the movement of God's Spirit within us. They are like glimpses of heaven, glimpses of beauty and peace. It is easy to dismiss these moments as products of our dreams or poetic imagination. But when we choose to claim them as God's way of tapping us on our shoulders and showing us the deepest truth of our existence, we can gradually step beyond our need to judge others and our inclination to evaluate everybody and everything. Then we can grow toward real inner freedom and real sanctity.

But—we can only let go of the heavy burden of judging others when we don't mind carrying the light burden of being judged![19]

On Worry

People often say: "Don't worry, things will work out fine." But we do worry and we can't stop worrying just because someone tells us to. One of the painful things of life is that we worry a great deal about our children, our friends, our spouse, our job, our future, our family, our country, our world, and endless other things. We know the answer to Jesus' question: "Can any of you, however much you worry, add a single cubit to your span of life?" (Matthew 6:27). We know that our worrying does not help us, nor does it solve any of our problems. Still, we worry a lot and, therefore, suffer a lot. We wish that we could stop worrying, but we don't know how. Even though we realize that, tomorrow, we may have forgotten what we were worrying about so much today, we still find it impossible to turn off our anxious minds. Can we do anything to worry less and be more at peace? If it is true that we cannot change anything by worrying about it, how then can we train our hearts and minds not to waste time and energy with anxious ruminations that make us spin around inside ourselves? Jesus says: "set your heart on God's kingdom first." That gives us a hint as to the right direction.[20]

"Look at the birds in the sky. They do not sow or reap or gather into barns; yet your heavenly Father feeds them. Are you not worth much more than they are? . . . Set your hearts on the kingdom first, and on God's saving justice, as well. So do not worry about tomorrow; tomorrow will take care of itself."
—Matthew 6:26, 33-4

Who Is to Blame?

Walking on the streets of New York City, Boston, Toronto, Paris, Amsterdam, or Rome, I don't see many radiant, joy-filled faces. Most people look tired. Their eyes stare away into empty space or are cast down to the ground. They carry newspapers in their hands that speak about corruption, blackmail, crime, violence, war, and impending catastrophes. Their burdens are heavy, their yokes very hard. With their whole being they cry out: "Why do we live and why do we keep living?"[21]

As he went along, he saw a man who had been blind from birth. His disciples asked him, "Rabbi, who sinned, this man or his parents, that he should have been born blind?"
—*John 9:1-2*

Confronting the Human Dilemma

To the question who was to blame for the tragedy of a man born blind, Jesus replied, "Nobody. He was born blind so that God's works might be revealed in him" (John 9:3).

We spend a lot of energy wondering who can be blamed for our own or other people's tragedies—our parents, ourselves, the immigrants, the Jews, the gays, the blacks, the fundamentalists, the Catholics? There is a strange satisfaction in being able to point our finger at someone, even ourselves. It gives us some sort of explanation and offers us some form of clarity.

But Jesus doesn't allow us to solve our own or other people's problems through blame. The challenge he poses is to discern in the midst of our darkness the light of God. In Jesus' vision everything, even the greatest tragedy, can become an occasion in which God's works can be revealed.

How radically new my life would be if I were willing to move beyond blaming to proclaiming the works of God in our midst. I don't think it has much to do with the exterior of life. All human beings have their tragedies—death, depression, betrayal, rejection, poverty, separation, loss, and so on. We seldom have much control over them. But do we choose to live them as occasions to blame, or as occasions to see God at work?

The whole Hebrew Bible is a story of human tragedies, but when these tragedies are lived and remembered as the context in which God's unconditional love for the people of Israel is revealed, this story becomes sacred history.[22]

An Example of Scapegoating Oneself

Living a daily routine in a house with handicapped people brings us in direct confrontation with our resistance to living our suffering as a way to glory. For me this is a daily reality. One of our handicapped men, Raymond, has, after many years in an institution, defined himself as the guilty one. He simply cannot believe that there is anything good in him and thus has become incapable of giving thanks. When I say, "Good morning, Raymond," he says, "I am not awake yet." When I say, "I will miss you when you are gone for the weekend," he says, "I won't miss you for sure." When I call him long distance to say hello, he says, "Don't bug me, I am eating." When I bring him a nice gift, he says, "My room is too full for new things." It is not easy to live with such a voice close by, but it is the voice of our broken world saying: "You are to blame for your suffering. You got what you deserved and if you got a broken body or a broken mind, you are the one who is the guilty one." The endless chain of Raymond expressing self-rejection, self-blame, shame, and guilt brings the challenge of the new teaching of the risen Lord right into the heart of our life together.

Once, after a long litany of negativism, I shouted at Raymond in desperation, saying: "But Raymond, you are a good man." And with a most emphatic voice he shouted back: "No, no I am not!" And suddenly I realized that he was clinging to his deep sense of guilt as the only way to make sense out of his immense suffering. All the violence that rips our world apart became suddenly visible in the "No, no I am not!" shouted by my own brother.

Raymond is such an important member of our family. I see my own guilt, shame, and self-rejection in his anguished face. I hear my own self-complaints, self-accusations, and self-condemnation in his screams and I cannot run away. It is not the hiddenness of Adam or the intimate friendship of Bill that is the greatest challenge to my spiritual growth, but the merciless self-flagellation of Raymond who cannot believe that the sting has been taken out of death and who makes me realize that I still do not believe it either.[23]

He looked up and said, "Woman, where are they? Has no one condemned you?" "No one, sir" she replied. "Neither do I condemn you," Jesus said.
—John 8:10-1

Seeking the Kingdom

God wants my heart to be totally given to the first love, so that I will really trust God and give everything away. I'm still not able to do that. I say, "Leave your father, leave your mother, leave your brother, leave your sister, leave your possessions, leave your success. Don't cling to friends. Trust that God will give you all you need." But do I really believe it?[24]

Think how the flowers grow; they never have to spin or weave; yet, . . . not even Solomon in all his royal robes was clothed like one of them. Now if that is how God clothes a flower which is growing wild today and is thrown into the furnace tomorrow, how much more will he look after you . . . ? But you must not set your hearts on things to eat and things to drink; nor must you worry. It is the gentiles of the world who set their hearts on all these things. Your Father well knows you need them. No; set your hearts on his kingdom, and these other things will be given to you as well.
—Luke 12:27-31

What Should We Care Most About?

The words of Jesus, "set your hearts on God's kingdom first . . . and all other things will be given you as well," summarize best the way we are called to live our lives. With our hearts set on God's kingdom. That kingdom is not some faraway land that we hope to reach, nor is it life after death or an ideal state of affairs. No. God's kingdom is, first of all, the active presence of God's spirit within us, offering us the freedom we truly desire.

And so the main question becomes: How to set our hearts on the kingdom first when our hearts are preoccupied with so many things? Somehow a radical change of heart is required, a change that allows us to experience the reality of our existence from God's place.

Once I saw a mime in which a man was straining to open one of the three doors in the room where he found himself. He pushed and pulled at the doorknobs, but none of the doors would open. Then he kicked with his feet against the wooden panels of the door, but they didn't break. Finally, he threw his full weight against the doors, but none of them yielded.

It was a ridiculous, yet very hilarious sight, because the man was so concentrated on the three locked doors that he didn't even notice that the room had no back wall and that he could simply walk out if he would only turn around and look!

That is what conversion is all about. It is a complete turnaround that allows us to discover that we are not the prisoners we think we are. From God's place, we often look like the man who tries to open the locked doors of his room. We worry about many things and even wound ourselves while worrying. God says: "Turn around, set your heart on my kingdom. I give you all the freedom you desire."[25]

"Martha," he said, "you worry and fret about so many things, and yet few are needed, indeed only one."—John 10:41

The Mystery of Obedience and Transformation

Jesus' advice to set our hearts on God's kingdom is somewhat paradoxical. You might give it the following interpretation: "If you want to worry, worry about that which is worth the effort. Worry about larger things than your family, your friends, or tomorrow's meeting. Worry about the things of God: truth, life, and light!"

As soon, however, as we set our hearts on these things our minds stop spinning because we enter into communion with the One who is present to us Here and Now and is there to give us what we most need. And so worrying becomes prayer, and our feelings of powerlessness are transformed into a consciousness of being empowered by God's spirit.

Indeed, we cannot prolong our lives by worrying, but we can move far beyond the boundaries of our short life span and claim eternal life as God's beloved children.

Does that put an end to our worrying? Probably not. As long as we are in our world, full of tensions and pressures, our minds will never be free from worries, but when we keep returning with our hearts and minds to God's embracing love, we will be able to keep smiling at our own worrisome selves and keep our eyes and ears open for the sights and sounds of the kingdom.

From Mind to Heart

How do we concretely go about setting our hearts on God's kingdom? When I lay in my bed, not able to fall asleep because of my many worries, when I do my work preoccupied about all the things that can go wrong, when I can't get my mind off my concern for a dying friend— what am I supposed to do? Set my heart on the kingdom? Fine, but how does one do this?

There are as many answers to this question as there are people with different lifestyles, personalities, and external circumstances. There is not one specific answer that fits everyone's needs. But there are some answers that can offer helpful directions.

One simple answer is to move from the mind to the heart by slowly saying a prayer with as much attentiveness as possible. This may sound like offering a crutch to someone who asks you to heal his broken leg. The truth, however, is that a prayer, prayed from the heart, heals. When you know the Our Father, the Apostles' Creed, the Glory Be to the Father by heart, you have something to start with. You might like to learn by heart the Twenty-third Psalm: "The Lord is my shepherd . . ." or Paul's words about love to the Corinthians or St. Francis's prayer: "Lord, make me an instrument of your peace . . ." As you lie in your bed, drive your car, wait for the bus, or walk your dog, you can slowly let the words of one of these prayers go through your mind simply trying to listen with your whole being to what they are saying. You will be constantly distracted by your worries, but if you keep going back to the words of the prayer, you will gradually discover that your worries become less obsessive and that you really start to enjoy praying. And as the prayer descends from your mind into the center of your being you will discover its healing power.

Nothing Is Wanting!

Why is the attentive repetition of a well-known prayer so helpful in setting our hearts on the kingdom? It is helpful because the words of such a prayer have the power to transform our inner anxiety into inner peace.

For a long time, I prayed the words, "The Lord is my shepherd; there is nothing I shall want. Fresh and green are the pastures where he gives me repose. Near restful waters he leads me to revive my drooping spirit." I prayed these words in the morning for half an hour sitting quietly on my chair trying only to keep my mind focused on what I was saying. I prayed them during the many moments of the day when I was going here or there, and I even prayed them during my routine activities. The words stand in stark contrast to the reality of my life. I want many things; I see mostly busy roads and ugly shopping malls; and if there are any waters to walk along they are mostly polluted. But as I keep saying: "The Lord is my shepherd . . ." and allow God's shepherding love to enter more fully into my heart, I become more fully aware that the busy roads, the ugly malls, and the polluted waterways are not telling the true story of who I am. I do not belong to the powers and principalities that rule the world but to the Good Shepherd who knows his own and is known by his own. In the presence of my Lord and Shepherd there truly is nothing I shall want. He will, indeed, give me the rest my heart desires and pull me out of the dark pits of my depression.

It is good to know that millions of people have prayed these same words over the centuries and found comfort and consolation in them. I am not alone when I pray these words. I am surrounded by countless women and men, those who are close by and those who are far away, those who are presently living and those who have died recently or long ago, and I know that long after I have left this world these same words will continue to be prayed until the end of time. The deeper these words enter into the center of my being, the more I become part of God's people and the better I understand what it means to be in the world without being of it.[26]

"I am the good shepherd; I know my own and my own know me, just as the Father knows me and I know the Father; and I lay down my life for the sheep."
—John 10:14-5

The Prayer of the Pharisee

There has been so much individualism, competition, rivalry, privileges, favors, and exceptions in my way of living that few deep and lasting bonds could grow. But Jesus came to create bonds, and living in, with, and through Jesus means discovering these bonds in myself and revealing them to others.[27]

Two men went up to the Temple to pray, one a Pharisee and the other a tax collector. —Luke 18:10

Jesus Challenges Our Arrogance

In one of Jesus' stories a Pharisee, standing by himself, prays to God: "God, I thank you that I am not like other people" (Luke 18:11).

That's a prayer we often pray. "I'm glad I'm not like him, her, or them. I am lucky not to belong to that family, that country, or that race. I am blessed not to be part of that company, that team, or that crowd!" Most of this prayer is unceasing! Somewhere we are always comparing ourselves with others, trying to convince ourselves that we are better off than they are. It is a prayer that wells up from our fearful selves and guides many of our thoughts and actions.

But this is a very dangerous prayer. It leads from compassion to competition, from competition to rivalry, from rivalry to violence, from violence to war, from war to destruction. It is a prayer that lies all the time, because we are not the difference we try so hard to find. No, our deepest identity is rooted where we are like other people—weak, broken, sinful, but sons and daughters of God.

I even think that we should not thank God for not being like other creatures, animals, plants, or rocks! We should thank God that indeed we are like them, not for better or worse but integral parts of God's creation. This is what humility is all about. We belong to the humus, the soil, and it is in this belonging that we can find the deepest reason for gratitude. Our prayer must be, "Thank you, God, that I am worthy to be part of your creation. Be merciful to me a sinner." Through this prayer we will be justified (see Luke 18:14), that is, find our just place in God's Kingdom.[28]

The Rich Young Man

He was setting out on a journey when a man ran up, knelt before him and put this question to him, "Good master, what must I do to inherit eternal life?"

—Mark 10:17

Unable to Respond Fully at the Critical Moment

"Jesus looked steadily at him and loved him, and he said, 'There is one thing you lack, Go and sell everything you own and give the money to the poor, and you will have treasure in heaven; then come, follow me.' But his face fell at these words and he went away sad, for he was a man of great wealth" (Mark 10:21-2).

Jesus loved this young man and, as I understand it, desired to have him with him as a disciple. But the young man's life was too complex; he had too many things to worry about, too many affairs to take care of, too many people to relate to. He couldn't let go of his concerns, and thus, disappointed and downcast, he left Jesus.[30]

I feel like praying tonight that my life might become simple enough for me to be able to say "yes" when Jesus looks at me with love and invites me to leave everything behind and follow him. Missing that moment would not only sadden Jesus and me but would, in a way, also be a refusal to take my true place in God's work of salvation.[31]

Perhaps There Is More to the Story

This story does not imply a huge leap from everything to nothing but rather a long series of small steps in the direction of love. The tragedy for the rich young man was not that he was unwilling to give up his wealth—who would be? The real tragedy for him was that he missed something both he and Jesus desired, which was the opportunity to develop a deep and intimate relationship. It

Only when we come in touch with our own life experiences and have learned to listen to our inner cravings for liberation and new life can we realize that Jesus did not just speak, but that he reached out to us in our most personal needs. The Gospel doesn't just contain ideas worth remembering. It is a message responding to our individual human condition.[29]

"In truth I tell you, there is no one who has left house, brothers, sisters, mother, father, children or land for my sake and for the sake of the gospel who will not receive a hundred times as much. . . Many who are first will be last, and the last, first."—Mark 10:29-30,31

Detail of *The washing of the feet.*

is not so much a question of detachment as it is a question of fully trusting and following the voice of love. Detachment is only a consequence of a greater attachment. Who would worry about his few possessions when invited to be intimate with the Lord of abundance, who offers more fish than we can catch and more bread than we can eat? What would have happened if the young man had said yes to Jesus? Wouldn't he, just like the other disciples, have become a source of hope for countless people? Now he drops out of history and is never heard of again! What a loss! To follow the voice of love, step by step, trusting that God will give us all we need, is the great challenge.[32]

The Loaves and the Fishes

Jesus climbed the hillside and sat down there with his disciples. The time of the Jewish Passover was near. Looking up, Jesus saw the crowds approaching and said to Philip, "Where can we buy some bread for these people to eat?"

—John 6:3-5

The Lord is so good. Brothers and sisters, when you hold on to what you have, it always gets less. When you give away what little you have, it always multiplies, whether it is food or knowledge or affection or love.[33]

Large Results from Small Offerings

Being at L'Arche helps one to understand the Gospels in a new way. Today we read the story of the multiplication of bread. "Looking up, Jesus saw the crowds approaching and said to Philip, 'Where can we buy some bread for these people to eat?' . . . Andrew said, 'Here is a boy with five barley loaves and two fish; but what is that among so many?'" (John 6:5-9). For Jesus, the small gifts of an insignificant boy were enough to feed everyone and even have twelve large baskets with scraps left over.

This again is a story about the value of the small people and the small things. The world likes things to be large, big, impressive, and elaborate. God chooses the small things which are overlooked in the big world. Andrew's remark, "five barley loaves and two fish; but what is that among so many?" captures well the mentality of a calculating mind. It sounds as if he says to Jesus, "Can't you count? Five loaves and two fish are simply not enough." But for Jesus they were enough. Jesus took them and gave thanks. That means that he received the small gifts from the small people and acknowledged them as gifts from his heavenly Father. What comes from God must be enough for all the people. Therefore, Jesus distributed the loaves and the fish "as much as they wanted." In giving away the small gifts from the small people, God's generosity is revealed. There is enough, plenty even, for everyone—there are even many leftovers. Here a great mystery becomes visible. What little

"I am the bread of life. No one who comes to me will ever hunger; no one who believes in me will ever thirst."—John 6:35

we give away multiplies. This is the way of God. This is also the way we are called to live our lives. The little love we have, the little knowledge we have, the little advice we have, the little possessions we have, are given to us as gifts of God to be given away. The more we give them away, the more we discover how much there is to give away. The small gifts of God all multiply in the giving.

Something of that mystery is becoming clear to me at L'Arche. How little is L'Arche! The few hundred handicapped people who are cared for in the L'Arche foyers all over the world seem a tiny, insignificant group, considering the countless handicapped people who remain without the necessary care. Statistically, L'Arche makes little sense. And still, something of God is taking place through L'Arche. The little that L'Arche does affects people from the most different countries, religions, races, and social backgrounds. Many are fed by the little food L'Arche is giving away, not just mentally handicapped people, but also the rich, the powerful, the leaders of the church and the society, students, scholars, doctors, lawyers, magistrates, businessmen and women, and people who do not even know what a mental handicap is. They all receive something from L'Arche and are strengthened by it. Thus the miracle of the multiplication of bread continues. It is just a question of having an eye for it.[34]

The Sending of the Disciples

He called the Twelve together and gave them power and authority over all devils and to cure diseases, and he sent them out to proclaim the kingdom of God and to heal. He said to them, "Take nothing for the journey: neither staff, nor haversack, nor bread, nor money; and do not have a spare tunic."

—Luke 9:1-3

Traveling Together

When Jesus speaks about shepherding, he does not want us to think about a brave, lonely shepherd who takes care of a large flock of obedient sheep. In many ways he makes it clear that ministry is a communal and mutual experience.

First of all, Jesus sends the twelve out in pairs (Mark 6:7). We keep forgetting that we are being sent out two by two. We cannot bring good news on our own. We are called to proclaim the Gospel together, in community. There is a divine wisdom here. "If two of you on earth agree to ask anything at all, it will be granted to you by my Father in heaven. For where two or three meet in my name, I am there among them" (Matthew 18:19-20). You might already have discovered for yourself how radically different traveling alone is from traveling together. I have found over and over again how hard it is to be truly faithful to Jesus when I am alone. I need my brothers and sisters to pray with me, to speak with me about the spiritual task at hand, and to challenge me to stay pure in mind, heart and body. But far more importantly, it is Jesus who heals, not I; Jesus who speaks words of truth, not I; Jesus who is Lord, not I. This is very clearly made visible when we proclaim the redeeming power of God together. Indeed, whenever we minister together, it is easier for people to recognize that we do not come in our own name, but in the name of the Lord Jesus who sent us.

I am deeply aware of my own tendency to want to go from communion to ministry without forming community. My individualism and desire for personal success ever and again tempt me to do it alone and claim the task of ministry for myself. But Jesus himself didn't preach and heal alone. Luke the Evangelist tells us how he spent the night in communion with God, the morning to form community with the twelve apostles, and the afternoon to go out with them ministering to the crowds.[35]

In the past I traveled a lot, preaching and giving retreats as well as commencement and keynote addresses. But I always went alone. Now, however, every time I am sent by the community to speak somewhere, the community tries to send me with a companion. Being with Bill is a concrete expression of the vision that we should not only live in community, but also minister in community. Bill and I are sent by our community in the conviction that the same Lord who binds us together in love will also reveal himself to us and others as we walk together on the road.[36]

Detail of *Jesus saves Peter from drowning.* London, British Museum/Art Resource, NY

Jesus Walks upon the Sea

And at once he made the disciples get into the boat and go on ahead to the other side while he sent the crowds away. After sending the crowds away he went up into the hills by himself to pray. When evening came he was there alone, while the boat, by now some furlongs from land, was hard pressed by rough waves, for there was a head-wind. In the fourth watch of the night he came towards them, walking on the sea, and when the disciples saw him walking on the sea, they were terrified. "It is a ghost," they said, and cried out in fear. But at once Jesus called out to them, saying, "Courage! It's me! Don't be afraid."

—Matthew 14:22-7

A Teaching on Fear

Why is there no reason to fear any longer? Jesus himself answers this question succinctly when he approaches his frightened disciples walking on the lake: "It is I. Do not be afraid" (John 6:20). The house of love is the house of Christ, the place where we can think, speak, and act in the way of God—not in the way of a fear-filled world. From this house the voice of love keeps calling out: "Do not be afraid . . . come and follow me . . . see where I live . . . go out and preach the good news . . . the kingdom of God is close at hand . . . there are many rooms in my Father's house. Come . . . take for your heritage the Kingdom prepared for you since the foundation of the world."

The house of love is not simply a place in the afterlife, a place in heaven beyond this world. Jesus offers us this house right in the midst of our anxious world.[38]

Letting Go of Fear

When I was in Latin America and lived among the poor

Hardly a day passes in our lives without our experience of inner and outer fears, anxieties, apprehensions, and preoccupations. These dark powers have pervaded every part of our world to such a degree that we can never fully escape them. Still it is possible not to belong to those powers, not to build our dwelling place among them, but to choose the house of love as our home.[37]

Jesus put out his hand at once and held him. "You have so little faith," he said, "why did you doubt?"
—Matthew 14:31

and oppressed people, I suddenly started to realize that they were not fearful people. Where I noticed hunger and oppression, torture and agony, I found more gratitude, more joy, more peace, and less fear than among those who have so many more of the world's goods. Suddenly I realized that the other side of oppression, the other side of the poverty of the South, is the fear and the guilt and the loneliness and the anguish in the North. Somehow those two can never be separated. Our suffering, which is often fear and loneliness and anguish and lack of freedom, is not separated from the oppression and from the poverty and from the anguish of those who live in what we call Third World countries.

But Jesus speaks to us in the Gospel with very strong words. Throughout the Gospel, we hear, "Do not be afraid." That is what Gabriel says to Mary. That is what the angels say to the women at the tomb: "Do not be afraid." And that is what the Lord himself says when he appears to his disciples: "Do not be afraid, it is I. Do not be afraid, it is I. Fear is not of God. I am the God of love, a God who invites you to receive—to receive the gifts of joy and peace and gratitude of the poor, and to let go of your fears so that you can start sharing what you are so afraid to let go of."

The invitation of Christ is the invitation to move out of the house of fear and into the house of love: to move out of that place of imprisonment into a place of freedom. "Come to me, come to my house which is a house of love," Jesus says.[39]

Finding Meaning in Our Life and Times

For nothing is hidden but it will be made clear, nothing secret but it will be made known and brought to the light. So take care how you listen. —Luke 8:17-8

Once we start reading the events of our time as calls to conversion, our perception of history changes radically.[40]

Invitation to Conversion

In our ongoing search for meaning, we need to keep reading books and newspapers in a spiritual way. The question that should always be with us is: "Why are we living?" All the events of our short lives need to be interpreted. Books and newspapers are there to help us to read the signs of the times and so give meaning to our lives. Jesus says: "When you see a cloud looming up in the West you say at once that rain is coming, and so it does. And when the wind is from the South you say it's going to be hot, and it is. Hypocrites! You know how to interpret the face of the earth and the sky. How is it you do not know how to interpret these times?" (Luke 12:54-6).

Here lies the real challenge. Jesus does not look at the events of our times as a series of incidents and accidents that have little to do with us. Jesus sees the political, economic, and social events of our life as signs that call for a spiritual interpretation. They need to be read spiritually! But how? Jesus shows us how. Once the people had told Jesus the news that the governor Pilate had executed some rebellious men from Galilee and mingled their blood with that of Roman sacrifices. When he heard this he said: "Do you suppose that these Galileans were worse sinners than any others, that this should happen to them? They were not, I tell you. No, but unless you repent you will all perish as they did" (Luke 13:2-3). Jesus does not give a political interpretation of the event but a spiritual one. He says: "What happened invites you to conversion!" This is the deepest meaning of history: a constant invitation calling us to turn our hearts to God and so discover the full meaning of our lives.[41]

God's Questions

Were the Jews who were killed in the gas chambers of the Nazi concentration camps more guilty than we are? What about the Maya Indians in Guatemala who were kidnapped, tortured, and executed by the military and the millions of Africans who starved to death . . . ? And what about those who did the killing?

These are the questions from below, the questions we raise when we want to figure out who is better or worse than we are. But these are not the questions from above. These are not God's questions. God does not ask us to define our little niche in humanity over and against other people. God's question is: are you reading the signs of your time as signs asking you to repent and be converted? What really counts is our willingness to let the immense sufferings of our brothers and sisters free us from all arrogance and from all judgments and condemnations and give us a heart as gentle and humble as the heart of Jesus.

We spend countless hours making up our minds about others. An unceasing exchange of opinions about people close by or far away keeps us distracted and allows us to ignore the truth that we ourselves are the first ones who need a change of heart and probably the only ones whose hearts we indeed can change.

We always say again: "What about him? What about her?" What Jesus says to us, as he said to Peter, who wanted to know what would happen to John: "What does it matter to you? You are to follow me" (John 21:21-2).[42]

Can We See Christ?

There is one question left. It may prove to be the most important one. "Can we see Christ in the world?" The answer is "No, we cannot see Christ in the world, but only through the Christ in us can we see Christ in the world." The answer reveals that the Christ within us opens our eyes to the Christ among us. That is what is meant by the expression "spirit speaks to Spirit." It is the Spirit of the living Christ dwelling in our innermost being who gives us eyes to contemplate the living Christ as he becomes visible in the concrete events of our history.[43]

"You know that among the gentiles those they call their rulers lord it over them, and their great men make their authority felt. Among you this is not to happen. No; anyone who wants to become great among you must be your servant . . . For the Son of man himself came not to be served but to serve, and to give his life as a ransom for many."
—Mark 10:42-5

"Whoever drinks this water will be thirsty again; but no one who drinks the water that I shall give will ever be thirsty again: the water that I shall give will become a spring of water within, welling up for eternal life."—John 4:13-4

Jesus with the woman at the well. Amsterdam, Rijksprentenkabinet

The Woman at the Well

When a Samaritan woman came to draw water, Jesus said to her, "Give me something to drink." His disciples had gone into the town to buy food. The Samaritan woman said to him, "You are a Jew. How is it that you ask me, a Samaritan, for something to drink?"—Jews, of course, do not associate with Samaritans. Jesus replied to her: "If you only knew what God is offering and who it is that is saying to you, 'Give me something to drink,' you would have been the one to ask, and he would have given you living water."

"You have no bucket, sir," she answered, "and the well is deep."   *—John 4:7-11*

Jesus Sees Her Truly

Jean Vanier explained to me once how Jesus recognized the sterility of the woman at the well. Jesus met her at noon, when it is very hot and nobody comes to the well to fetch water. She came at that time because she did not dare join the town's women, who came early in the morning not only for water, but also for the latest news. She was an outcast not welcome among her own. When Jesus said to her, "The water that I shall give will turn into an inner spring" (John 4:14), he confronted her with her spiritual sterility and offered her healing. At the end of the story we see how this rejected, fearful woman returns to her town and testifies fearlessly: "Come and see a man who has told me everything I ever did; I wonder if he is the Christ?" (John 4:29). She is freed of her fear, she is healed of her sterility, and she has become a fruitful witness of the life-giving Christ.[45]

Jesus Transforms the Question by His Answer

A careful look at the gospels shows that Jesus seldom

Do not despair, thinking that you cannot change yourself after so many years. Simply enter into the presence of Jesus as you are and ask him to give you a fearless heart where he can be with you. You cannot make yourself different, Jesus came to give you a new heart, a new spirit, a new mind, and a new body. Let him transform you by his love and so enable you to receive his affection in your whole being.[44]

Detail of *Jesus with the woman at the well.*

accepted the questions posed to him. He exposed them as coming from the house of fear. "Who is the greatest in the kingdom of heaven? How often must I forgive my brother if he wrongs me? Is it against the law for a man to divorce his wife on any pretext whatever? What authority do you have for acting like this? At the resurrection, to which of those seven [men she married] will she be a wife, since she had been married to them all? Are you the king of the Jews? Lord, has the hour come? Are you going to restore the kingdom to Israel?. . ." To none of these questions did Jesus give a direct answer. He gently put them aside as questions emerging from false worries. They were raised out of concern for prestige, influence, power, and control. They did not belong to the house of God. Therefore Jesus always transformed the question by his answer. He made the question new—and only then worthy of his response.

Though we think of ourselves as followers of Jesus, we are often seduced by the fearful questions the world presents to us. Without fully realizing it, we become anxious, nervous, worrying people caught in the questions of survival: our own survival, the survival of our families, friends, and colleagues, the survival of our church, our country, and our world. Once these fearful survival questions become the guiding questions of our lives, we tend to dismiss words spoken from the house of love as unrealistic, romantic, sentimental, pious, or just useless. When love is offered as an alternative to fear we say: "Yes, yes, that sounds beautiful, but . . ." The "but" reveals how much we live in the grip of the world, a world which calls Christians naïve and raises "realistic" questions: "Yes, but what if you grow old and there is nobody to help you? Yes, but what if you lose your job and you have no money to take care of yourself and your family? Yes, but what if refugees come to this country by the millions and disrupt the ways we have been living for so long?"

When we raise these "realistic" questions we echo a cynical spirit which says: "Words about peace, forgiveness, reconciliation, and new life are wonderful but the real issues cannot be ignored. They require that we do not allow others to play games with us, that we retaliate when we are offended, that we are always ready for war, and never let anyone take away the good life we have so carefully built up for ourselves." But as soon as these so-called "real issues" begin to dominate our lives, we are back again in the house of fear, even though we keep borrowing words of love, and continue to experience vague desires to live in the house of love.[46]

The woman said to him, "I know that Messiah—that is Christ—is coming; and when he comes he will explain everything." Jesus said, "That is who I am, I who speak to you."
—John 4:25-6

Welcoming the Child

Jesus does not ask me to remain a child but to become one. Becoming a child is living toward a second innocence: not the innocence of the newborn infant, but the innocence which is reached through conscious choices.[47]

At this time the disciples came to Jesus and said, "Who is the greatest in the kingdom of Heaven?" So he called a little child to him whom he set among them. Then he said, "In truth I tell you, unless you change and become like little children you will never enter the kingdom of Heaven. And so, the one who makes himself as little as this little child is the greatest in the kingdom of Heaven."
—Matthew 18:1-4

Jesus Was Not Just Speaking about Little Children

"Anyone who welcomes a little child such as this in my name, welcomes me; and anyone who welcomes me, welcomes not me but the one who sent me" (Mark 9:37).

What does welcoming a little child mean? It means giving loving attention to those who are often overlooked. I imagine myself standing in line to meet a very important person and noticing a little child passing by. Would I leave the line and pay all my attention to this child? I imagine myself going to a grand party where I will meet very interesting and powerful people. Could I forget about the party to sit on the street for a few hours with a man who stretches out his hands and asks me for some money? I imagine myself being invited to receive an award. Could I let the honor go to spend the time with a depressed, elderly woman who is forgotten by her friends and feels isolated in her apartment?

Yesterday I was stopped on the street by a beggar. He asked me for some change to buy a bite to eat. He didn't expect any response, but when I gave him ten dollars he jumped up and said, "Thank you, thank you very, very much." He was extremely surprised by this large gift, but I suddenly felt a deep sadness. I was on my way to a meeting I did not want to miss. My gift was an excuse for walk-

ing on. I had not welcomed the beggar—I had just tried to feel generous. My "generosity" had revealed my deep resistance toward welcoming the "little child."

To welcome the "little child" I have to become little myself. But I continue to wonder how great I am. Even my generosity can help me feel great. But Jesus said, "If anyone wants to be first, he must make himself last of all" (Mark 9:35). Am I willing to become the servant of this beggar? By giving him ten dollars I became his master, who could make him say, "Thank you, thank you very much."

It is becoming clear to me that I still have not understood that Jesus revealed his love to us by becoming our servant, and calls us to follow him in this way.[48]

Detail of *The good Samaritan looks after the wounded man.*

Entering the Kingdom Like a Child

This morning I wondered what the Gospel reading would be. Often I have the feeling that the Gospel of the day will tell me all I have to know.

I read, "Let the little children come to me; do not stop them; for it is to such as these that the kingdom of God belongs. In truth I tell you, anyone who does not welcome the kingdom of God like a little child will never enter it" (Mark 10:14-5).

What is so special about a little child? The little child has nothing to prove, nothing to show, nothing to be proud of. All the child needs to do is receive the love that is offered. Jesus wants us to receive the love he offers. He wants nothing more than that we allow him to love us and enjoy that love. This is so hard since we always feel that we have to deserve the love offered to us. But Jesus wants to offer that love to us not only because we earned it, but because he has decided to love us independently of any effort on our side. Our own love for each other should flow from that "first love" that is given to us undeserved.

Regarding Simple People as One's Teachers

As I was reflecting on Jesus' words, I started to see more clearly how Daybreak could help me not only to receive the little children, but also to become like one of them. The handicapped may be able to show me the way to a second childhood. Indeed, they can reveal to me God's first love. Handicapped people have little, if anything, to show to the world. They have no degrees, no reputation, no influence, no connections with influential people. They do not create much, produce much, or earn much. They have to trust that they can receive and give pure love. I have already received so many hugs and kisses here from people who have never heard of me and are not the least impressed by me that I have to start believing that the love they offer is freely given, to be freely received.

My dream is that Daybreak can increasingly become a place where the first love of God is revealed to people anxious to prove they deserve love. A house of prayer and welcome, in which handicapped people could receive guests searching for God, might be a concrete way to exercise the ministry of that first love.[49]

⊸ Entering the Heart ⊷
of the Gospel

The good Samaritan looks after the wounded man.
Berlin, Kupferstichkabinett der Staatliche Museen/Art Resource, NY

Peter Realizes Who Jesus Is

When Jesus came to the region of Caesarea Philippi he put this question to his disciples, "Who do people say the Son of man is?" And they said, "Some say John the Baptist, some Elijah, and others Jeremiah or one of the prophets." "But you," he said, "who do you say that I am?" Then Simon Peter spoke up and said, "You are the Christ, the Son of the living God."

—*Matthew 16:13-6*

We Are Church

When you can say to Jesus, "You are the Messiah, the Son of the living God," Jesus can say to you, "You are the rock on whom I will build my church." There is a mutuality of recognition and a mutuality of truth here. When we acknowledge that God has come among us through the Messiah—his anointed one—to free us from our captivity, God can point to our solid core and make us the foundation for a community of faith.

Our "rock" quality will be revealed to us when we confess our need for salvation and healing. We can become community builders when we are humble enough to see our dependence on God.

It is sad that the dialogue between Jesus and Simon Peter has, in my church, been almost exclusively used to explain the role of the papacy. By doing so, it seems to me that we miss seeing that this exchange is for all of us. We all have to confess our need for salvation, and we all have to accept our solid center.

And the keys of the Kingdom? They too belong first to all who confess Jesus as their Christ and thus come to belong to a community of faith in which our binding and unbinding happen in the Name of God. When indeed the body of Christ, formed by believers, makes decisions about

I'm profoundly convinced that the greatest spiritual danger for our times is the separation of Jesus from the Church. The Church is the body of the Lord. Without Jesus there can be no Church; and without the Church we cannot stay united to Jesus. I've yet to meet anyone who has come closer to Jesus by forsaking the Church.[1]

its members, these are Kingdom decisions. That is what Jesus refers to when he says, "Whatever you bind on earth will be bound in heaven, and whatever you loose on earth will be loosed in heaven" (Matthew 16:19).

These thoughts came to my mind on this Feast of the Chair of St. Peter, as we were gathering around the table with several people who had left the Catholic Church because they saw it as too authoritarian. More than ever it is important to realize that the Church is not simply "over there," where the bishops are or where the Pope is, but "right here," where we are around the table of the Lord.[2]

Living Stones

He is the living stone, rejected by human beings but chosen by God and precious to him; set yourselves close to him so that you, too, may be living stones making a spiritual house as a holy priesthood to offer the spiritual sacrifices made acceptable to God through Jesus Christ. As scripture says: "Now, I am laying a stone in Zion, a chosen, precious cornerstone and no one who relies on this will be brought to disgrace." —1 Peter 2:4-6

Predictions of the Passion

Then he began to teach them that the Son of man was destined to suffer grievously, and to be rejected by the elders and the chief priests and the scribes, and to be put to death, and after three days to rise again; and he said all this quite openly. Then, taking him aside, Peter tried to rebuke him. —Mark 8:31-2

The Sign of Jesus

Jesus' attitude to suffering and death was quite different from ours. For him, they were realities he encountered with his eyes wide open. Actually, his whole life was a conscious preparation for them. Jesus doesn't commend suffering and death as desirable things; but he does speak of them as something we ought not to repudiate, avoid, or cover up.

On a number of occasions he foretold his own suffering and death. Quite soon after Jesus had commissioned his twelve disciples, he was already telling them: "The Son of Man is destined to suffer grievously, to be rejected by the elders and chief priests and scribes and to be put to death, and to be raised up on the third day." Not so long after, he repeated this prophecy with the words: "You must have these words constantly in mind: The Son of Man is going to be delivered into the power of men." That even in those days they wanted to ignore reality is surely evident from Peter's reaction. "Then, taking him aside, Peter started to rebuke him. 'Heaven preserve you, Lord,' he said, 'This must not happen to you.'" Jesus' reply is cutting. It would even appear that he regards Peter's reaction as the most dangerous of all for those in quest of a truly spiritual life: "Get behind me, Satan! You are an obstacle in my path, because you are thinking not as God thinks but as human beings do." After that, he tells his disciples yet again, and very

"Those who lose their life for my sake will find it," Jesus says. There is no day without many losses. If we are attentive to our inner life, we quickly realize how many times things are not happening in the way we hoped, people aren't saying what we expected, the day is not evolving as we wanted, et cetera, et cetera. All these little "losses" can make us bitter people who complain that life is not fair to us. But if we live these losses for the sake of Jesus—that is, in communion with his redemptive death—then our losses can gradually free us from our self-centeredness and open our hearts to the new life that comes from God. The real question is: "Do I live my losses for my sake or for Jesus' sake?" That choice is a choice for death or life.[3]

They were on the road, going up to Jerusalem; Jesus was walking on ahead of them; they were in a daze, and those who followed were apprehensive. Once more taking the Twelve aside he began to tell them what was going to happen to him.—Mark 10:32

plainly, that a person wanting to lead a spiritual life cannot do so without the prospect of suffering and death. Living spiritually is made possible only through a direct, uncushioned confrontation with the reality of death. Just listen to what Jesus has to say: "If anyone wants to be a follower of mine, let him renounce himself and take up his cross and follow me. Anyone who wants to save his life will lose it; but anyone who loses his life for my sake will find it."

Finding new life through suffering and death: that is the core of the good news. Jesus has lived out that liberating way before us and has made it the great sign. Human beings are forever wanting to see signs: marvelous, extraordinary, sensational events that can distract them a little from hard reality. It isn't without reason that we keep on looking among the stars to see whether they are stars of earth or stars of heaven. We would like to see something marvelous, something exceptional, something that interrupts the ordinary life of every day. That way, if only for a moment, we can play at hide-and-seek. But to those who say to Jesus: "Master, . . . we should like to see a sign from you," he replies: "It is an evil and unfaithful generation that asks for a sign! The only sign it will be given is the sign of the prophet Jonah. For as Jonah remained in the belly of the sea monster for three days and three nights, so will the Son of Man be in the heart of the earth for three days and three nights."

From this you can see what the authentic sign is; not some sensational miracle but the suffering, death, burial, and resurrection of Jesus. The great sign, which can be understood only by those who are willing to follow Jesus, is the sign of Jonah, who also wanted to run away from reality but was summoned back by God to fulfill his arduous task to the end. To look suffering and death straight in the face and to go through them oneself in the hope of a new God-given life: that is the sign of Jesus and of every human being who wishes to lead a spiritual life in imitation of him. It is the sign of the cross: the sign of suffering and death, but also of the hope for total renewal.[4]

Teaching in Parables

Then the disciples went to him and asked, "Why do you talk to them in parables?"

In answer he said, "Because to you is granted to understand the mysteries of the kingdom of Heaven, but to them it is not granted. Anyone who has will be given more and will have more than enough; but anyone who has not will be deprived even of what he has. The reason I talk to them in parables is that they look without seeing and listen without hearing or understanding. So in their case what was spoken by the prophet Isaiah is being fulfilled:

Listen and listen, but never understand!
Look and look, but never perceive!

—Matthew 13:10-4

Jesus as Storyteller

First of all, let's keep in mind the context in which Jesus tells the parables, like the story of the "man who had two sons." Luke writes: "The tax collectors and sinners . . . were all crowding around to listen to him, and the Pharisees and scribes complained saying: 'This man welcomes sinners and eats with them.'" They put his legitimacy as a teacher in question by criticizing his closeness to sinful people. In response Jesus tells his critics the parables of the lost sheep, the lost coin, and the prodigal son.

Jesus wants to make it clear that the God of whom he speaks is a God of compassion who joyously welcomes repentant sinners into his house. To associate and eat with people of ill repute, therefore, does not contradict his teaching about God, but does, in fact, live out this teaching in everyday life. If God forgives the sinners, then certainly those who have faith in God should do the same. If God welcomes sinners home, then certainly those who trust in

In the Gospels, "to see" and "to hear" are among the most used words. Jesus says to his disciples, "blessed are your eyes because they see, your ears because they hear! In truth I tell you, many prophets and upright people longed to see what you see, and never saw it; to hear what you hear, and never heard it" (Matthew 13:16-7). Seeing and hearing God are the greatest gifts we can receive. Both are ways of knowing, but all through the scriptures I sense that seeing God is the most intimate and personal of the two.[5]

God should do likewise. If God is compassionate, then certainly those who love God should be compassionate as well. The God whom Jesus announces and in whose name he acts is the God of compassion, the God who offers himself as example and model for all human behavior.

But there is more. Becoming like the heavenly Father is not just one important aspect of Jesus' teaching, it is the very heart of his message. The radical quality of Jesus' words and the seeming impossibility of his demands are quite obvious when heard as part of a general call to become and to be true sons and daughters of God.

As long as we belong to this world, we will remain subject to its competitive ways and expect to be rewarded for all the good we do. But when we belong to God, who loves us without conditions, we can live as he does. The great conversion called for by Jesus is to move from belonging to the world to belonging to God.[6]

Jesus spoke to the crowds in parables; indeed, he would never speak to them except in parables. This was to fulfill what was spoken by the prophet: "I will speak to you in parables, unfold what has been hidden since the foundation of the world."   —Matthew 13:34-5

Drinking the Cup

Then the mother of Zebedee's sons came with her sons to make a request of him, and bowed low; and he said to her, "What is it you want?" She said to him, "Promise that these two sons of mine may sit one at your right hand and the other at your left in your kingdom." Jesus answered, "You do not know what you are asking. Can you drink the cup that I am going to drink?" They replied, "We can." —Matthew 20:20-2

The question now is: How do we drink the cup of salvation? We have to drink our cup slowly, tasting every mouthful—all the way to the bottom! Living a complete life is drinking our cup until it is empty, trusting that God will fill it with everlasting life.[7]

Swallowing All of Life

When Jesus asks his friends James and John, the sons of Zebedee, "Can you drink the cup that I am going to drink?" he poses the question that goes right to the heart of my priesthood and my life as a human being. Years ago, when I held the beautiful golden chalice in my hands, that question didn't seem hard to answer. For me, a newly ordained priest full of ideas and ideals, life seemed to be rich with promises. I was eager to drink the cup!

Today, sitting in front of a low table surrounded by men and women with mental disabilities and their assistants, and offering them the glass cups of wine, that same question has become a spiritual challenge. Can I, can we, drink the cup that Jesus drank?

I still remember the day, a few years ago, when the story in which Jesus raises that question was read during the Eucharist. It was 8:30 in the morning, and about twenty members of the Daybreak community were gathered in the little basement chapel. Suddenly the words "Can you drink the cup?" pierced my heart like the sharp spear of a hunter. I knew at that moment—as with a flash of insight—that taking this question seriously would radically change our lives. It is the question that has the power to crack open a hardened heart and lay bare the tendons of the spiritual life.

"Can you drink the cup? Can you empty it to the dregs? Can you taste all the sorrows and joys? Can you live your life to the full whatever it will bring?" I realized these were our questions.

But why should we drink this cup? There is so much pain, so much anguish, so much violence. Why should we drink the cup? Wouldn't it be a lot easier to live normal lives with a minimum of pain and a maximum of pleasure?

After the reading, I spontaneously grabbed one of the large glass cups standing on the table in front of me and looking at those around me—some of whom could hardly walk, speak, hear, or see—I said: "Can we hold the cup of life in our hands? Can we lift it up for others to see, and can we drink it to the full?" Drinking the cup is much more than gulping down whatever happens to be in there, just as breaking bread is much more than tearing a loaf apart. Drinking the cup of life involves holding, lifting, and drinking. It is the full celebration of being human.

Can we hold our life, lift our life, and drink it, as Jesus did? In some of those around me, there was a sign of recognition, but in myself there was a deep awareness of truth. Jesus' question had given me a new language with which to speak about my life and the lives of those around me. For a long time after that simple morning Eucharist, I kept hearing Jesus' question: "Can you drink the cup that I am going to drink?" Just letting that question sink in made me feel very uncomfortable. But I knew that I had to start living with it.[8]

The Raising of Lazarus

There was a man named Lazarus of Bethany, the village of Mary and her sister, Martha, and he was ill. It was the same Mary, the sister of the sick man Lazarus, who anointed the Lord with ointment and wiped his feet with her hair. The sisters sent this message to Jesus, "Lord, the man you love is ill." On receiving the message, Jesus said, "This sickness will not end in death, but it is for God's glory so that through it the Son of God may be glorified." —John 11:1-4

Lazarus, Come Out!

Walk and don't be afraid. Don't want to have it all charted out for you. Let it happen. Let something new grow. That is the walk of faith—walking with the Lord, always walking away from familiar places. "Leave your father, leave your mother, leave your brother, leave your sister. Follow me. I am the Lord of love." And wherever there is love, fear will be wiped out. "Perfect love casts out all fear."

You can go out and you will live. You will live eternally because Jesus is the Lord of life. That is the ecstasy. You can start participating in it every time you step out of your fear and out of the sameness. It doesn't require big jumps, but simply small steps.[10]

A Story with Many Layers

The resurrection of Lazarus is one of the most complex stories of the New Testament. It has many levels of meaning. This morning I found myself speaking about it without always knowing on which level I was moving.

First of all, there is the contrast between the death threat against Jesus and the calling to life of Lazarus. When Jesus says to his disciples, "Lazarus is dead. For your sake I

Jesus said, "Live ecstatically. Move out of that place of death and toward life because I am the God who is living. Wherever I am, there is life, there is change, there is growth, there is increase and blossoming and something new. I am going to make everything new."

For us to dare to live a life in which we continue to move out of the static places and take trusting steps in new directions— that is what faith is all about. The Greek word for faith means to trust—to trust that the ground before you that you never walked on is safe ground, God's ground, holy ground.[9]

"I am the resurrection. Anyone who believes in me, even though that person dies, will live, and whoever lives and believes in me will never die."—John 11:25

am glad I was not there, so that you may believe. But let us go to him," Thomas says to his fellow disciples, "Let us also go, that we may die with him" (John 11:14-6). Going to Lazarus meant going to Judea, where Jesus' enemies were trying to kill him. But going to Lazarus also meant going to the place of life. The resurrection of Lazarus becomes the event where death and life touch each other. After Lazarus was called back to life, the leaders became determined to kill Jesus (John 11:53). All of this can be seen as Jesus' way to prepare his friends and disciples for his own death and resurrection. By resurrecting Lazarus, Jesus shows that he is indeed the resurrection (John 11:25) and that his own death, which will happen soon, is not a final death.

Second, there is a love story here. Lazarus was one of Jesus' closest friends, and his deep compassion for Lazarus's sisters, as well as his great love for Lazarus, moved Jesus to call Lazarus back to life. Whenever Jesus calls someone to life—the son of the widow Nain, the daughter of Jairus—we always see an immense love and compassion. It is this love and compassion that is the source of new life.

Third, there are Jesus' words when he first heard of Lazarus's illness: "This illness does not lead to death; rather it is for God's glory, so that the Son of God may be glorified through it" (John 11:4). As in many other situations Jesus sees a tragic event as the opportunity to reveal God's glory.

How do all these levels belong together? Maybe the best way to answer that question is to look at Jesus' own death and resurrection. There we see that the final power of death is overcome. There we see that this overcoming of death takes place in the context of love of those who know Jesus intimately. There we see the greatest tragedy of human history become the occasion for the salvation of the world.[11]

Entry into Jerusalem

Then they took the colt to Jesus and threw their cloaks on his back, and he mounted it. Many people spread their cloaks on the road, and others greenery which they had cut in the fields. And those who went in front and those who followed after were all shouting, "Hosanna! Blessed is he who comes in the name of the Lord! Blessed is the coming kingdom of David our father! Hosanna in the highest heavens!"   —Mark 11:7-10

Jesus on a Donkey

Christ on a Donkey, in the Augustiner Museum in Freiburg, is one of the most moving Christ figures I know. I have sent many postcards of it to my friends, and I keep one in my prayer book.

This afternoon I went to the museum to spend some quiet time with this *Christus auf Palmesel* (Christ on palm-donkey). This fourteenth-century sculpture originally comes from Niederrotweil, a small town close to Breisnach on the Rhine. It was made to be pulled on a cart in the Palm Sunday procession. In 1900 it was sold to the Augustiner Museum, where it now stands in the center of the first exposition hall.

Christ's long, slender face with the high forehead, inward-looking eyes, long hair, and a small forked beard expresses the mystery of his suffering in a way that holds me spellbound. As he rides into Jerusalem surrounded by people shouting "hosanna," "cutting branches from the trees and spreading them in his path" (Matthew 21:8), Jesus appears completely concentrated on something else. He does not look at the excited crowd. He does not wave. He sees beyond the noise and movement to what is ahead of him: an agonizing journey of betrayal, torture, crucifixion, and death. His unfocused eyes can see what nobody

Jesus spoke with great authority, but his whole life was complete obedience to his Father, and Jesus, who said to his Father, "Let it be as you, not I, would have it" (Matthew 26:39), has been given all authority in heaven and on earth (see Matthew 28:18). Let us ask ourselves: Do we live our authority in obedience and do we live our obedience with authority? We usually think of people with great authority as higher up, far away, hard to reach. But spiritual authority comes from compassion and emerges from deep inner solidarity with those who are "subject" to authority. The one who is fully like us, who deeply understands our joys and pains or hopes and desires, and who is willing and able to walk with us, that is the one to whom we gladly give authority and whose "subjects" we are willing to be.[12]

around him can see; his high forehead reflects a knowledge of things to come far beyond anyone's understanding.

There is melancholy, but also peaceful acceptance. There is insight into the fickleness of the human heart, and also immense compassion. There is a deep awareness of the unspeakable pain to be suffered, but also a strong determination to do God's will. Above all, there is love, an endless, deep, and far-reaching love born from an unbreakable intimacy with God and reaching out to all people, wherever they are, were, or will be. There is nothing that he does not fully know. There is nobody whom he does not fully love.

Every time I look at this Christ on the donkey, I am reminded again that I am seen by him with all my sins, guilt, and shame and loved with all his forgiveness, mercy and compassion.

Just being with him in the Augustiner Museum is a prayer. I look and look and look, and I know that he sees the depths of my heart; I do not have to be afraid.[13]

Detail of *Jesus finds the disciples sleeping in the garden.*

Washing the Disciples' Feet

Before the festival of the Passover, Jesus, knowing that his hour had come to pass from this world to the Father, having loved those who were his in the world, loved them to the end.

They were at supper, and the devil had already put it into the mind of Judas Iscariot, son of Simon, to betray him. Jesus knew that the Father had put everything into his hands, and that he had come from God and was returning to God, and he got up from table, removed his outer garments and, taking a towel, wrapped it round his waist; he then poured water into a basin and began to wash the disciples' feet and to wipe them with the towel he was wearing. —John 13:1-5

It is in union with the body of Christ that I come to know the full significance of my own body. My body is much more than a mortal instrument of pleasure and pain. It is a home where God wants to manifest the fullness of the divine glory. The loving care given to our bodies and the bodies of others is therefore a truly spiritual act, since it leads the body closer to its glorious existence.[14]

The Master Kneels before Us

The Word became flesh so as to wash my tired feet. He touches me precisely where I touch the soil, where earth connects with my body that reaches out to heaven. He kneels and takes my feet in his hands and washes them. Then he looks up at me and, as his eyes and mine meet, he says: "Do you understand what I have done for you? If I, your Lord and Master, have washed your feet, you must wash your brothers' and sisters' feet" (John 13:13-4). As I walk the long, painful journey toward the cross, I must pause on the way to wash my neighbors' feet. As I kneel before my brothers and sisters, wash their feet, and look into their eyes, I discover that it is because of my brothers and sisters who walk with me that I can make the journey at all.[15]

Washing the Feet of the Poor

This afternoon I took the train to Paris to celebrate the Holy Thursday liturgy with the L'Arche community,

The washing of the feet.
Amsterdam, Rijksprentenkabinet

"Nomaste." It was a very moving celebration. We gathered in the community room of Nomaste. There were about forty people. In his welcome, the director of the community, Toni Paoli, expressed his vision that L'Arche should be not simply a comfortable place for handicapped people, but a Christian community in which people serve one another in the name of Jesus. After the Gospel reading, he again proclaimed his deep love for Jesus. Then he stood up and washed the feet of four members of his community.

After the Eucharist, a rice dish, bread, and wine were brought and put on the altar. In silence, deepened by three short Gospel readings about God's love, we shared this simple food.

Sitting in the basement room in Paris surrounded by forty poor people, I was struck again by the way Jesus concluded his active life. Just before entering on the road of his passion he washed the feet of his disciples and offered them his body and blood as food and drink. These two acts belong together. They are both an expression of God's determination to show us the fullness of his love. Therefore John introduces the story of the washing of the disciples' feet with the words: "Jesus . . . having loved those who were his in the world, loved them to the end" (John 13:1).

What is even more astonishing is that on both occasions Jesus commands us to do the same. After washing his disciples' feet, Jesus says, "I have given you an example so that you may copy what I have done to you" (John 13:15). After giving himself as food and drink, he says, "Do this in remembrance of me" (Luke 22:19). Jesus calls us to continue his mission of revealing the perfect love of God in this world. He calls us to total self-giving. He does not want us to keep anything for ourselves. Rather, he wants our love to be as full, as radical, and as complete as his own. He wants us to bend ourselves to the ground and touch the places in each other that most need washing. He also wants us to say to each other, "Eat of me and drink of me." By this complete mutual nurturing, he wants us to become one body and one spirit, united by the love of God.

When Toni spoke to his community about his love for Jesus, and when I saw how he washed their feet and gave them the bread and wine, it seemed as if—for the moment—I saw a glimpse of the new kingdom Jesus came to bring. Everybody in the room knew how far he or she was from being a perfect expression of God's love. But everybody was also willing to make a step in the direction to which Jesus pointed.

It was an evening in Paris I will not easily forget.[16]

"At this moment you do not know what I am doing, but later you will understand." "Never!" said Peter. "You shall never wash my feet." Jesus replied, "If I do not wash you, you can have no share with me."
—John 13:7-8

The Last Supper

Isn't a meal together the most beautiful expression of our desire to be given to each other in our brokenness? The table, the food, the drinks, the words, the stories: are they not the most intimate ways in which we not only express the desire to give ourselves to each other, but also do this in actuality?[17]

He sent two of his disciples, saying to them, "Go into the city and you will meet a man carrying a pitcher of water. Follow him, and say to the owner of the house where he enters, 'The Master says: Where is the room for me to eat the Passover with my disciples?' He will show you a large upper room furnished with couches, all prepared."

—Mark 14:13-5

In the Eucharist, Jesus Gives All

Every time we invite Jesus into our homes, that is to say, into our life with all its light and dark sides, and offer him the place of honor at our table, he takes the bread and the cup and hands them to us saying: "Take and eat, this is my body. Take and drink, this is my blood. Do this to remember me." Are we surprised? Not really! Wasn't our heart burning when he talked to us on the road? Didn't we already know that he was not a stranger to us? Weren't we already aware that the one who was crucified by our leaders was alive and with us? Hadn't we seen it before, that he took the bread, blessed it, broke it, and gave it to us? He did so before the large crowd who had listened for long hours to his word, he did it in the upper room before Judas handed him over to suffering, and he has done it countless times when we have come to the end of a long day and he joins us around the table for a simple meal.

The Eucharist is the most ordinary and the most divine gesture imaginable. That is the truth of Jesus. So human, yet so divine; so familiar, yet so mysterious; so close, yet so revealing! But that is the story of Jesus who "being in the form of God did not count equality with God something to be grasped, but emptied himself, taking the form of a slave, becoming as human beings are; and being in every way like a human being, he was humbler yet, even to accepting

The Last Supper. New York, The Metropolitan Museum of Art

death, death on a cross" (Philippians 2:6-8). It is the story of God who wants to come close to us, so close that we can see him with our own eyes, hear him with our own ears, touch him with our own hands; so close that there is nothing between us and him, nothing that separates, nothing that divides, nothing that creates distance.

Jesus is God-for-us, God-with-us, God-within-us. Jesus is God giving himself completely, pouring himself out for us without reserve. Jesus doesn't hold back or cling to his own possessions. He gives all there is to give. "Eat, drink, this is my body, this is my blood . . . , this is me for you!"

We all know of this desire to give ourselves at the table. We say: "Eat and drink; I made this for you. Take more; it is there for you to enjoy, to be strengthened, yes, to feel how much I love you." What we desire is not simply to give food, but to give ourselves. "Be my guest," we say. And as we encourage our friends to eat from our table, we want to say, "Be my friend, be my companion, be my love—be part of my life—I want to give myself to you."

In the Eucharist, Jesus gives all. The bread is not simply a sign of his desire to become our food; the cup is not just a sign of his willingness to be our drink. Bread and wine become his body and blood in the giving. The bread, indeed, is his body given for us; the wine his blood poured out for us. As God becomes fully present for us in Jesus, so Jesus becomes fully present to us in the bread and the wine of the Eucharist. God not only became flesh for us years ago in a country far away. God also becomes food and drink for us now at this moment of the Eucharistic celebration, right where we are together around the table. God does not hold back; God gives all. That is the mystery of the Incarnation. That too is the mystery of the Eucharist. Incarnation and Eucharist are the two expressions of the immense, self-giving love of God. And so the sacrifice on the cross and the sacrifice at the table are one sacrifice, one complete, divine self-giving that reaches out to all humanity in time and space.

The word that best expresses this mystery of God's total self-giving love is "communion." It is the word that contains the truth that, in and through Jesus, God wants, not only to teach us, instruct us, or inspire us, but to become one with us. God desires to be fully united with us so that all of God and all of us can be bound together in a lasting love. The whole long history of God's relationship with us human beings is a history of ever-deepening communion. It is not simply a history of unities, separations, and restored unities, but a history in which God searches for ever-new ways to commune intimately with those created in God's own image.[18]

Betrayal by One of the Twelve

Jesus was deeply disturbed and declared, "In all truth I tell you, one of you is going to betray me." The disciples looked at each other, wondering whom he meant. The disciple whom Jesus loved was reclining next to Jesus; Simon Peter signed to him and said, "Ask him who it is he means," so, leaning back close to Jesus' chest he said, "Who is it, Lord?" Jesus answered, "It is the one to whom I give the piece of bread that I dip in the dish." And when he had dipped the piece of bread he gave it to Judas son of Simon Iscariot. At that instant, after Judas had taken the bread, Satan entered him. Jesus then said, "What you are going to do, do quickly." —*John 13:21-7*

God Handed Jesus Over

Jesus, sitting at table with his disciples, said, "One of you will betray me" (John 13:21). I read this today in the Gospel.

As I look more closely at Jesus' words as they are written in Greek, a better translation would be "One of you will hand me over." The term *paradidomi* means "to give over, to hand over, to give into the hands of." It is an important term not only to express what Judas did, but also what God did. Paul writes, ". . . he did not spare his own Son, but 'handed him over' for the sake of all of us" (Romans 8:32).

If we translate Judas' action "to betray," as applied to Judas, we do not fully express the mystery because Judas is described as being an instrument of God's work. That is why Jesus said, "The Son of Man is going to his fate, as the scriptures say he will, but alas for the man by whom the Son of Man is betrayed [handed over]" (Matthew 26:24).

This moment when Jesus is handed over to those who do with him as they please is a turning point in Jesus' ministry. It is turning from action to passion. After years of

It seems that there are more and more people in our society who have less and less influence on the decisions that affect their own existence. Therefore, it becomes increasingly important to recognize that the largest part of our existence involves waiting in the sense of being acted upon. But the life of Jesus tells us that not to be in control is part of the human condition. His vocation was fulfilled not just in action but also in passion, in waiting.[19]

Detail of *The Last Supper.*

teaching, preaching, healing, and moving to wherever he wanted to go, Jesus is handed over to the caprices of his enemies. Things are now no longer done by him, but to him. He is flagellated, crowned with thorns, spat at, laughed at, stripped, and nailed naked to a cross. He is a passive victim, subject to other people's actions. From the moment Jesus is handed over, his passion begins, and through this passion he fulfills his vocation.

It is important for me to realize that Jesus fulfills his mission not by what he does, but by what is done to him. Just as with everyone else, most of my life is determined by what is done to me and thus is passion. And because most of my life is passion, things being done to me, only small parts of my life are determined by what I think, say, or do. I am inclined to protest against this and to want all to be action, originated by me. But the truth is that my passion is a much greater part of my life than my action. Not to recognize this is self-deception and not to embrace my passion with love is self-rejection.

It is good news to know that Jesus is handed over to passion, and through his passion accomplishes his divine task on earth. It is good news for a world passionately searching for wholeness.

Jesus' words to Peter remind me that Jesus' transition from action to passion must also be ours if we want to follow his way. He says, "When you were young you put on your own belt and walked where you liked; but when you grow old you will stretch out your hands, and somebody else will put a belt round you and take you where you would rather not go" (John 21:18).

I, too, have to let myself be "handed over" and thus fulfill my vocation.[20]

The Farewell Discourse

"Do not let your hearts be troubled. You trust in God, trust also in me. In my Father's house there are many places to live in; otherwise I would have told you. I am going now to prepare a place for you, and after I have gone and prepared you a place, I shall return to take you to myself."

—John 14:1-3

"I Am the True Vine, and My Father Is the Vinedresser"

Jesus said, "I am the true vine, and my Father is the vinedresser. Every branch in me that bears no fruit he cuts away, and every branch that does bear fruit he prunes, to make it bear even more" (John 15:1-2).

These words in today's Gospel open a new perspective on suffering for me. Pruning helps trees to bear more fruit. Even when I bear fruit, even when I do things for God's kingdom, even when people express gratitude for coming to know Jesus through me, I need a lot more pruning. Many unnecessary branches and twigs prevent the vine from bearing all the fruit it can. They have to be clipped off. This is a painful process, all the more so because I do not always know that they are unnecessary. They often seem beautiful, charming, and very alive. But they need to be cut away so that more fruit can grow.

It helps me to think about painful rejections, moments of loneliness, feelings of inner darkness and despair, and lack of support and human affection as God's pruning. I am aware that I might have settled too soon for the few fruits that I can recognize in my life. I might say, "Well, I am doing some good here and there, and I should be grateful for and content with the little good I do." But that might be false modesty and even a form of spiritual laziness. God calls me to more. God wants to prune me. A pruned vine does not look beautiful, but during harvest time it pro-

In Jesus, God became one of us to lead us through Jesus into the intimacy of his divine life. Jesus came to us to become as we are and left us to allow us to become as he is. By giving us his Spirit, his breath, he became closer to us than we are to ourselves. It is through this breath of God that we can call God "Abba, Father," and can become part of the mysterious divine relationship between Father and Son.[21]

duces much fruit. The greatest challenge is to continue to recognize God's pruning hand in my life. Then I can avoid resentment and depression and become even more grateful that I am called upon to bear even more fruit than I thought I could. Suffering then becomes a way of purification and allows me to rejoice in its fruits with deep gratitude and without pride.[22]

"Abide in My Love"

Jesus says, "If you keep my commandments, you will abide in my love, just as I have kept my Father's commandments and abide in God's love" (John 15:10). Jesus invites me to abide in his love. That means to dwell with all that I am in him. It is an invitation to a total belonging, to full intimacy, to an unlimited being-with.

Detail of *The Last Supper.*

The anxiety that has plagued me during the last week shows that a great part of me is not yet "abiding" in Jesus. My mind and heart keep running away from my true dwelling place, and they explore strange lands where I end up in anger, resentment, lust, fear, and anguish. I know that living a spiritual life means bringing every part of myself home to where it belongs.

Jesus describes the intimacy that he offers as the connectedness between the vine and its branches. I long to be grafted onto Jesus as a branch onto the vine so that all my life comes from the vine. In communion with Jesus, the vine, my little life can grow and bear fruit. I know it, but I do not live it. Somehow I keep living as if there are other sources of life that I must explore, outside of Jesus. But Jesus keeps saying, "Come back to me, give me all your burdens, all your worries, fears, and anxieties. Trust that with me you will find rest." I am struggling to listen to that voice of love and to trust in its healing power.

I deeply know that I have a home in Jesus, just as Jesus has a home in God. I know, too, that when I abide in Jesus I abide with him in God. "Those who love me," Jesus says, "will be loved by my Father" (John 14:21). My true spiritual work is to let myself be loved, fully and completely, and to trust that in that love I will come to the fulfillment of my vocation. I keep trying to bring my wandering, restless, anxious self home, so that I can rest there in the embrace of love.[23]

"I have told you this so that my own joy may be in you and your joy be complete. This is my commandment; love one another, as I have loved you. No one can have greater love than to lay down his life for his friends."
—John 15:11-3

"I Pray That They May Be One"

Jesus prays for unity among his disciples and among those who through the teaching of his disciples will come to believe in him. He says, "May they all be one, just as, Father, you are in me and I in you" (John 17:21).

These words of Jesus reveal the mystery that unity among people is not first of all the result of human effort, but rather a divine gift. Unity among people is a reflection of the unity of God. The desire for unity is deep and strong

"With me in them and you in me, may they be so perfected in unity that the world will recognize that it was you who sent me and that you have loved them as you have loved me."

—John 17:23

among people. It is a desire between friends, between married people, between communities, and between countries. Wherever there is a true experience of unity, there is a sense of giftedness. While unity satisfies our deepest need, it cannot be explained by what we say or do. There exists no formula for unity.

When Jesus prays for unity, he asks his Father that those who believe in him, that is, in his full communion with the Father, will become part of that unity. I continue to see in myself and others how often we try to make unity among ourselves by focusing all our attention on each other and trying to find the place where we can feel united. But often we become disillusioned, realizing that no human being is capable of offering us what we most want. Such disillusionment can easily make us become bitter, cynical, demanding, even violent.

Jesus calls us to seek our unity in and through him. When we direct our inner attention not first of all to each other, but to God to whom we belong, then we will discover that in God we also belong to each other. The deepest friendship is a friendship mediated by God; the strongest marriage bonds are bonds mediated by God.

This truth requires the discipline to keep returning to the source of all unity. If, in the midst of conflict, division, and discord, we would always try to enter together into the presence of God to find our unity there, much human suffering could be relieved.[24]

⇒ For This I Have Come ⇐

Prayer in the Garden

They came to a plot of land called Gethsemane and he said to his disciples, "Stay here while I pray." Then he took Peter and James and John with him. And he began to feel terror and anguish. And he said to them, "My soul is sorrowful to the point of death. Wait here, and stay awake." Then going on a little further he threw himself on the ground and prayed that, if it were possible, this hour might pass him by. "Abba, Father!" he said, "For you everything is possible. Take this cup away from me. But let it be as you, not I, would have it."

—*Mark 14:32-6*

The Cup of Sorrow Is Served

"Can you drink the cup that I am going to drink?" When Jesus brought this question to John and James, and when they impulsively answered with a big "We can," he made this terrifying, yet hope-filled prediction: "Very well; you shall drink my cup." The cup of Jesus would be their cup. What Jesus would live, they would live. Jesus didn't want his friends to suffer, but he knew that for them, as for him, suffering was the only and necessary way to glory. Later he would say to two of his disciples: "Was it not necessary that the Christ should suffer before entering into his glory?" (Luke 24:26). The "cup of sorrows" and the "cup of joys" cannot be separated. Jesus knew this, even though in the midst of his anguish in the garden, when his soul was "sorrowful to the point of death" (Matthew 26:38), he needed an angel from heaven to remind him of it. Our cup is often so full of pain that joy seems completely unreachable. When we are crushed like grapes, we cannot think of the wine we will become. The sorrow overwhelms us, makes us throw ourselves on the ground, face down, and sweat drops of blood. Then we need to be reminded that our cup

Today, O Lord, I felt intense fear. My whole being seemed to be invaded by fear. No peace, no rest, just plain fear: fear of mental breakdown, fear of living the wrong life, fear of rejection and condemnation, and fear of you. You, O Lord, have also known fear. You have been deeply troubled, your sweat and tears were the signs of your fear. Make my fear, O Lord, part of yours, so that it will lead me not to darkness but to the light, and will give me a new understanding of the hope of your cross.[1]

(opposite)
Detail of *Jesus finds the disciples sleeping in the garden.*
Berlin, Kupferstichkabinett Staatliche Museen

of sorrow is also our cup of joy and that one day we will be able to taste the joy as fully as we now taste the sorrow.[2]

Tabor and Gethsemane

Prayer . . . is far from sweet and easy. Being the expression of our greatest love, it does not keep pain away from us. Instead, it makes us suffer more since our love for God is a love for a suffering God and our entering into God's intimacy is an entering into the intimacy where all of human suffering is embraced in divine compassion. To the degree that our prayer has become the prayer of our heart we will love more and suffer more, we will see more light and more darkness, more grace and more sin, more of God and more of humanity. To the degree that we have descended into our heart and reached out to God from there, solitude can speak to solitude, deep to deep, and heart to heart. It is there where love and pain are found together.

On two occasions, Jesus invited his closest friends, Peter, John, and James, to share in his most intimate prayer. The first time he took them to the top of Mount Tabor, and there they saw his face shining like the sun and his clothes white as light (Matthew 17:2). The second time he took them to the garden of Gethsemane, and there they saw his face in anguish and his sweat falling to the ground like great drops of blood (Luke 22:44). The prayer of our heart brings us both to Tabor and Gethsemane. When we have seen God in glory we will also see God in misery, and when we have felt the ugliness of God's humiliation we also will experience the beauty of the transfiguration.[3]

The Arrest of Jesus

Judas, one of the Twelve, came up and with him a number of men armed with swords and clubs, sent by the chief priests and the scribes and elders. Now the traitor had arranged a signal with them, saying, "The one I kiss, he is the man." —Mark 14:43-4

The Passion Begins

The word "passion" is derived from the Latin verb *patior*, which means "to undergo." It is related to the word "passive."

Jesus' passion came after much action. For three years he went from village to village, town to town, preaching, teaching, responding to people's questions, healing the sick, confronting the hypocrites, consoling the sorrowing, calling the dead back to life. Wherever he went there were large crowds of people admiring him, listening to him, asking him for help. During these intense, nearly hectic years Jesus was in control of the situation. He came and went as he felt it was right for him to do. His disciples accepted his leadership and followed him wherever he went.

But at Gethsemane—the Garden of Olives—all this action came to a sudden end. There Jesus was handed over by one of his own disciples to undergo suffering. That's where his passion began. From that moment on he could no longer do anything; everything was done to him.[5]

The Resurrection Was Already Occurring

Resurrection is not just life after death. First of all, it is the life that bursts forth in Jesus' passion, in his waiting. The story of Jesus' suffering reveals that the resurrection is breaking through even in the midst of the passion. A crowd led by Judas came to Gethsemane. "Then Jesus . . . said to them, 'Whom do you seek?' They answered him, 'Jesus of

Jesus is arrested. The National Museum of Fine Arts, Stockholm.

Nazareth.' Jesus said to them, 'I am he' . . . When he said to them 'I am he,' they drew back and fell to the ground. Again he asked them, 'Whom do you seek?' And they said, 'Jesus of Nazareth.' Jesus answered, 'I told you that I am he; so, if you seek me, let these men go'" (John 18:4-8).

Precisely when Jesus is being handed over into his passion, he manifests his glory. "Whom do you seek? . . . I am he" are words which echo all the way back to Moses and the burning bush: "I am the one. I am who I am" (see Exodus 3:1-6). In Gethsemane, the glory of God manifested itself, and they fell flat on the ground. Then Jesus was handed over. But already in the handing over we see the glory of God who hands himself over to us. God's glory revealed in Jesus embraces passion as well as resurrection.

"The Son of Man," Jesus says, "must be lifted up as Moses lifted up the serpent in the desert, so that everyone who believes may have eternal life in him" (John 3:14-5). He is lifted up as a passive victim, so the Cross is a sign of desolation. And he is lifted up in glory, so the Cross becomes at the same time a sign of hope. Suddenly we realize that the glory of God, the divinity of God, bursts through in Jesus' passion precisely when he is most victimized. So new life becomes visible not only in the resurrection on the third day, but already in the passion, in the being handed over. Why? Because it is in the passion that the fullness of God's love shines through. It is supremely a waiting love, a love that does not seek control.

When we allow ourselves to feel fully how we are being acted upon, we can come in touch with a new life that we were not even aware was there. This was the question a sick friend and I talked about constantly. Could he taste the new life in the midst of his passion? Could he see that in his being acted upon by the hospital staff he was already being prepared for a deeper love? It was a love that had been underneath all the action, but he had not tasted it fully. So together we began to see that in the midst of our suffering and passion, in the midst of our waiting, we can already experience the resurrection.[6]

The Trial

➴

As you see more clearly that your vocation is to be a witness to God's love in this world, as you become more determined to live out that vocation, the attacks of the enemy will increase. You will hear voices saying, "You are worthless, you have nothing to offer, you are unattractive, undesirable, unlovable." Do not be afraid. The more you are called to speak for God's love, the more you will need to deepen the knowledge of that love in your own heart. The farther the outward journey takes you, the deeper the inner journey must be.[7]

The whole assembly then rose, and they brought him before Pilate. They began their accusation by saying, "We found this man inciting our people to revolt, opposing payment of the tribute to Caesar, and claiming to be Christ, a king." Pilate put to him this question, "Are you the king of the Jews?" He replied, "It is you who say it."

—Luke 23:1-3

God's Truth Was on Trial

Jesus stands before Pilate. He is silent. He does not defend himself against the many charges made against him. But when Pilate asks him, "What have you done?" he says, "I came into the world for this, to bear witness to the truth; and all who are on the side of truth listen to my voice" (John 18:35-7). The truth of which Jesus speaks is not a thesis, or a doctrine, or an intellectual explanation of reality. It is the very relationship, the life-giving intimacy between himself and the Father of which he wants us to partake. Pilate could not hear that, nor can anyone who is not connected to Jesus. Anyone, however, who enters into communion with Jesus will receive the Spirit of truth—the Spirit who frees us from the compulsions and obsessions of our contemporary society, who makes us belong to God's inner life, and allows us to live in the world with open hearts and attentive minds.

In communion with Jesus, we can hear the Spirit's voice and journey far and wide, whether we are in prison or not. Because the truth—the true relationship, the true belonging—gives us the freedom that the powers of darkness cannot take away. Jesus is the freest human being who ever lived because he was the most connected to God. Pilate condemned him. Pilate wanted to make him one of the damned. But he could not. Jesus' death, instead of being the execution of a death sentence, became the way to the full truth, leading to full freedom.

I know that the more I belong to God, the more I will be condemned. But the condemnation of the world will reveal the truth. "Blessed are those who are persecuted in the cause of uprightness, the kingdom of heaven is theirs" (Matthew 5:10). I have to trust these words. Precisely there where the world hates me, where I am not taken seriously by the powers that be, where I am pushed aside, laughed at and made marginal, there precisely I may discover that I am part of a worldwide community that is barred, fenced in, and locked away in isolated camps.

I hunger for the truth, for that communion with God that Jesus lived. But every time that hunger is satisfied, I will be condemned again and given a heavy cross to bear. It is the story of Peter and John, Paul and Barnabas, James and Andrew, and most of all of Mary, the mother of Jesus. Their joy and sorrow became one because they chose to live the truth in the world.[8]

"I was born for this, I came into the world for this, to bear witness to the truth; and all who are on the side of truth listen to my voice."
"Truth?" said Pilate. "What is that?"

—John 18:37-8

Jesus Is Scourged

There can be no human beings who are completely alone in their sufferings since God, in and through Jesus, has become Emmanuel, God with us. It belongs to the center of our faith that God is a faithful God, a God who did not want us to ever be alone but who wanted to understand—to stand under—all that is human. The Good News of the Gospel, therefore, is not that God came to take our suffering away, but that God wanted to become part of it.[9]

Pilate then had Jesus taken away and scourged; and after this, the soldiers twisted some thorns into a crown and put it on his head and dressed him in a purple robe. They kept coming up to him and saying, "Hail, King of the Jews!" and slapping him in the face. Pilate came outside again and said to them, "Look, I am going to bring him out to you to let you see that I find no case against him." Jesus then came out wearing the crown of thorns and the purple robe. Pilate said, "Behold the Man."[10]

—John 19:1-5

Jesus Suffers for All, Even for Me

Pilate handed Jesus over to be scourged. The soldiers "stripped him and put a scarlet cloak around him, and having twisted thorns into a crown, they put this on his head and placed a reed in his right hand. To make fun of him they knelt to him saying: Hail, King of the Jews!" And they spat on him and took the reed and struck him on the head with it. And when they had finished making fun of him, they took off the cloak and dressed him in his own clothes and led him away to crucifixion" (Matthew 27:28-31). Jesus undergoes it all. The time of action is past. He does not speak anymore; he does not protest; he does not reproach or admonish. He has become a victim. He no longer acts, but is acted upon. He has entered his passion. He knows that most of human life is passion. People are being starved, kidnapped, tortured, and murdered. People are being imprisoned, driven from their homes, separated from their families, put into camps, and used for slave labor. They do not know why. They do not understand the cause for it all. Nobody explains. They are poor. When Jesus felt the cross put on his shoulders, he felt the pain of all future generations pressing on him.

Detail of *Jesus is mocked.*

I feel powerless. I want to do something. I have to do something. I have, at least, to speak out against the violence and the malnutrition, the oppression and exploitation. Beyond this, I have to act in any way possible to alleviate the pain I see. But there is an even harder task: to carry my own cross, the cross of loneliness and isolation, the cross of the rejections I experience, the cross of my depression and inner anguish. As long as I agonize over the pain of others far away but cannot carry the pain that is uniquely mine, I may become an activist, even a defender of humanity, but not yet a follower of Jesus. Somehow my bond with those who suffer oppression is made real through my willingness to suffer my loneliness. It is a burden I try to avoid, sometimes, by worrying about others. But Jesus says, "Come to me, all you who labor and are overburdened, and I will give you rest" (Matthew 11:28). I might think that there is an unbridgeable gap between myself and the Guatemalan wood carrier. But Jesus carried his cross for both of us. We belong together. We must each take up our cross and follow him, and so discover that we are truly brothers who learn from him who is humble and gentle of heart. In this way only can a new humanity be born.[11]

The Road to Golgotha

➤

Every time I am willing to break out of my false need for self-sufficiency and dare to ask for help, a new community emerges—a fellowship of the weak-strong in the trust that together we can be people of hope for a broken world. Simon of Cyrene discovered a new communion. Everyone whom I allow to touch me in my weakness and help me to be faithful to my journey to God's home will come to realize that he or she has a gift to offer that may have remained hidden for a very long time.[12]

They led him out to crucify him. They enlisted a passer-by, Simon of Cyrene, father of Alexander and Rufus, who was coming in from the country, to carry his cross. They brought Jesus to the place called Golgotha, which means the place of the skull. —Mark 15:20-2

Taking Up the Cross of Jesus

When Jesus was carrying his cross to Golgotha, the soldiers came across a man from Cyrene, called Simon, and they enlisted him to carry the cross because it had become too heavy for Jesus alone. He was unable to carry it to the place of his execution and needed the help of a stranger to fulfill his mission. So much weakness, so much vulnerability. Jesus needs us to fulfill his mission. He needs people to carry the cross with him and for him. He came to us to show the way to his Father's home. He came to offer us a new dwelling place, to give us a new sense of belonging, to point us to the true safety. But he cannot do it alone. The hard, painful work of salvation is a work in which God becomes dependent on human beings. Yes, God is full of power, glory, and majesty. But God chose to be among us as one of us—as a dependent human being. To his followers who wanted to defend him with their swords Jesus said, "Put your sword back . . . . Or do you think that I cannot appeal to my Father, who would promptly send more than twelve legions of angels to my defense? But then, how would the Scriptures be fulfilled that say this is the way it must be?" (Matthew 26:52-4). Jesus' way is the way of powerlessness, of dependence, of passion. He who became a child, dependent on the love and care of Mary and Joseph and so many others, completes his earthly journey in total dependency. He becomes a waiting God. He waits, wondering what others will do with him. Will he be betrayed or

Jesus is given vinegar to drink on the cross.

proclaimed? Executed in abandonment or followed? Will he be nailed to the cross with no followers near him or will someone help him to carry the cross? For Jesus to become the savior of the world, he needs people willing to carry the cross with him. Some do it voluntarily; some have to be "enlisted"; but once they feel the weight of the wood, they discover that it is a light burden, an easy yoke that leads to the Father's home.[13]

Large numbers of people followed him, and women too, who mourned and lamented for him. . . When they reached the place called the Skull, there they crucified him and the two criminals, one on his right, the other on his left. Jesus said, "Father, forgive them; they do not know what they are doing."

—Luke 23:27,33-4

The Cross of Jesus

They offered him wine mixed with myrrh, but he refused it. Then they crucified him, and shared out his clothing, casting lots to decide what each should get. It was the third hour when they crucified him. The inscription giving the charge against him read, "The King of the Jews," and they crucified two bandits with him.

—Mark 15:23-7

Jesus, Suspended between Heaven and Earth

Jesus was nailed to the cross, and for three hours he was dying. He died between two men. One of them said to the other: "We are paying for what we did. But this man has done nothing wrong" (Luke 23:41). Jesus lived his dying completely for others. The total exhaustion of his body, the abandonment of his friends, and even of his God, all became the gift of self. And as he hung dying in complete powerlessness, nailed against the wood of a tree, there was no bitterness, no desire for revenge, no resentment. Nothing to cling to. All to give. "Unless a grain of wheat falls into the earth and dies, it remains only a single grain, but if it dies, it yields a rich harvest" (John 12:24). By being given away to others, his life became fruitful. Jesus, the complete innocent one, the one without sin, without guilt, without shame, died an excruciatingly painful death in order that death no longer would have to be ignored, but could become a gateway to life and the source of a new communion.[15]

Joining Our Voice to the Voice of the Crucified One

Handicapped people are not only poor; they also reveal to us our own poverty. Their primal call is an anguished cry: "Do you love me?" and "Why have you forsaken me?"

On the cross, Jesus has shown us how far God's love goes. It's a love which embraces even those who crucified him. When Jesus is hanging nailed to the cross, totally broken and stripped of everything, he still prays for his executioners. "Father, forgive them; they do not know what they are doing." Jesus' love for his enemies knows no bounds. He prays even for those who are putting him to death.[14]

(opposite)
Detail of *Jesus is given vinegar to drink on the cross.*

And when Jesus had cried out in a loud voice, he said, "Father, into your hands I commit my spirit."
—Luke 23:46

When we are confronted with that cry, so visible in those people who have no capacity to hide behind their intellectual defenses, we are forced to look at our own terrible loneliness and our own primal cry. We hear this cry everywhere in our world. Jews, blacks, Palestinians, refugees, and many others all cry out, "Why is there no place for us, why are we rejected, why are we pushed away?" Jesus has lived this primal cry with us. "My God, my God, why have you forsaken me?" He, who came from God to lead us to God, suffered the deepest anguish a human being can suffer, the anguish of being left alone, rejected, forgotten, abandoned by the one who is the source of all life.

L'Arche is founded on this cry of the poor. L'Arche is a response to the cry of Jesus, which is the cry of all who suffer anguish and who wonder if there can be any real bond with anyone.[16]

Death and Darkness

From the sixth hour there was darkness over all the land until the ninth hour. And about the ninth hour Jesus cried out in a loud voice, "Eli, eli, lama sabachthani?" that is, "My God, my God, why have you forsaken me?" When some of those who stood there heard this, they said, "The man is calling on Elijah," and one of them quickly ran to get a sponge and, putting it on a reed, gave it to him to drink. But the rest of them said, "Wait! And see if Elijah will come to save him." But Jesus, again crying out in a loud voice, yielded up his spirit.

—Matthew 27:45-50

The Light of the World Is Extinguished

Jesus died. The powers of death crushed him. Not only the fear-ridden judgments of Pilate, the torture by the Roman soldiers, and the cruel crucifixion, but also the powers and principalities of this world.[18] As we look at the dying Jesus, we see the dying world. Jesus, who on the cross drew all people to himself, died millions of deaths. He died not only the death of the rejected, the lonely, and the criminal, but also the death of the high and powerful, the famous and the popular. Most of all, he died the death of all the simple people who lived their ordinary lives and grew old and tired, and trusted that somehow their lives were not in vain.[19]

When we say "Christ has died," we express the truth that all human suffering in all times and places has been suffered by the Son of God who also is the Son of all humanity and thus has been lifted up into the inner life of God. There is no suffering—no guilt, shame, loneliness, hunger, oppression, or exploitation, no torture, imprisonment or murder, no violence or nuclear threat—that has not been suffered by God. All this has been said often

Becoming poor doesn't just mean forsaking house and family, having nowhere to lay one's head, and being increasingly persecuted; it also means parting company with friends, with success, and even with the awareness of God's presence. When, finally, Jesus is hanging on the cross and cries out with a loud voice, "My God, my God, why have you forsaken me?," only then do we know how far God has gone to show us his love. For it is then that Jesus not only reached his utmost poverty but also showed God's utmost love.[17]

before, but maybe not in a way that makes a direct connection with the agony of the world that we witness today. We have to come to the inner knowledge that the agony of the world is God's agony. The agony of women, men and children across the ages reveals to us the inexhaustible depth of God's agony that we glimpsed in the garden of Gethsemane. The deepest meaning of human history is the gradual unfolding of the suffering of Christ. As long as there is human history, the story of Christ's suffering has not yet been fully told. The more we try to enter into this mystery, the more we will come to see the suffering world as a world hidden in God. Outside of God human suffering is not only unbearable but cannot even be faced. But when we come to know the inner connectedness between the world's pain and God's pain, everything becomes radically different. Then we see that in and through Jesus Christ God has lifted up all human burdens into his own interiority and made them the way to recognize his immense love.[20]

Jesus is carried to the sepulchre. Berlin, Kupferstichkabinett der Staatliche Museen

Burial

And now a member of the Council arrived, a good and upright man named Joseph. He had not consented to what the others had planned and carried out. He came from Arimathaea, a Jewish town, and he lived in the hope of seeing the kingdom of God. This man went to Pilate and asked for the body of Jesus. He then took it down, wrapped it in a shroud and put it in a tomb which was hewn in stone and which had never held a body. It was Preparation day and the Sabbath was beginning to grow light.

Meanwhile the women who had come from Galilee with Jesus were following behind. They took note of the tomb and how the body had been laid. Then they returned and prepared spices and ointments. And on the Sabbath day they rested, as the Law required.

—Luke 23:50-6

Jesus is the Lord who came to save us by dying for us on the Cross. The wounds in Jesus' glorified body remind us of the way in which we are saved. But they also remind us that our own wounds are much more than roadblocks on our way to God. They show us our own unique way to follow the suffering Christ, and they are destined to become glorified in our resurrected life. Just as Jesus was identified by his wounds, so are we.[21]

Silent in the Earth

Joseph of Arimathaea placed the body of Jesus "in a tomb which was hewn in stone and which had never held a body . . . Meanwhile, the women who had come from Galilee with Jesus were following behind. They took note of the tomb and how the body had been laid. Then they returned and prepared spices and ointments. And on the Sabbath day they rested" (Luke 23:53-6).

There was deep rest around the grave of Jesus. On the seventh day, when the work of creation was completed, God rested. "God blessed the seventh day and made it holy, because on that day he rested after all his work of creating" (Genesis 2:3). On the seventh day of the week of our redemption, when Jesus had fulfilled all he was sent by his Father to do, he rested in the tomb, and the women whose hearts were broken with grief rested with him. Of all the days in history, Holy Saturday—the Saturday during which the body of Jesus lay in the tomb in silence and darkness behind the large stone that was rolled against its entrance (Mark 15:46)—is the day of God's solitude. It is the day on which no words are spoken, no proclamations made. The Word of God through whom all had been made lay buried in the darkness of the earth. This Holy Saturday is the most quiet of all days. Its quiet connects the first covenant with the second, the people of Israel with the not-yet-knowing world, the Temple with the new worship in the Spirit, the sacrifices of blood with the sacrifice of bread and wine, the Law with the Gospel. This divine silence is the most fruitful silence that the world has ever known. From this silence, the Word will be spoken again and make all things new. We have much to learn about God's resting in silence and solitude. It is a rest that has nothing to do with not being busy, although that might be a sign of it. The rest of God is a deep rest of the heart that can endure even as we are surrounded by the forces of death. It is the rest that offers us the hope that our hidden, often invisible existence will become fruitful even though we cannot say how and when.

It is the rest of faith that allows us to live on with a peaceful and joyful heart even when things are not getting better, even when painful situations are not resolved, even when revolutions and wars continue to disrupt the rhythm of our daily lives. This divine rest is known by all those who live their lives in the Spirit of Jesus. Their lives are not characterized by quietness, passivity, or resignation. On the contrary, they are marked by creative action for justice and peace. But that action comes forth from the rest of God in their hearts and is, therefore, free from obsession and compulsion, and rich in confidence and trust.

Whatever we do or do not do in our lives, we need always to remain connected with the rest of the Holy Saturday when Jesus lay buried in the tomb and the whole of creation waited for all things to be made new.[22]

❥ Death and Darkness ❧
Are Overcome

Mary of Magdala

Mary was standing outside the tomb, weeping. Then, as she wept, she stooped to look inside, and saw two angels in white sitting where the body of Jesus had been, one at the head, the other at the feet. They said, "Woman, why are you weeping?"

"They have taken my Lord away," she replied, "and I don't know where they have put him." As she said this she turned around and saw Jesus standing there, though she did not realize it was Jesus.　　　—*John 20:11-4*

Called by Name

Today we heard the story of the encounter between Jesus and Mary of Magdala, two people who love each other. Jesus says, "Mary." She recognizes him and says, "'Rabboni,' which means 'Master'" (John 20:16). This simple and deeply moving story brings me in touch with my fear as well as my desire to be known. When Jesus calls Mary by her name, he is doing much more than speaking the word by which everybody knows her, for her name signifies her whole being. Jesus knows Mary of Magdala. He knows her story: her sin and her virtue, her fears and her love, her anguish and her hope. He knows every part of her heart. Nothing in her is hidden from him. He knows her even more deeply and more fully than she knows herself. Therefore, when he utters her name he brings about a profound event. Mary suddenly realizes that the one who truly knows her truly loves her.

I am always wondering if people who know every part of me, including my deepest, most hidden thoughts and feelings, really do love me. Often I am tempted to think that I am loved only as I remain partially unknown. I fear that the love I receive is conditional and then say to myself, "If they really knew me, they would not love me." But when

The stranger reveals himself to us as the most intimate friend. When Mary of Magdala hears the stranger calling her by her name, she knows it is her Master. This knowing is much more than a simple recognition of a familiar person. It is a rediscovering of a long intimate relationship which has grown during years of listening, speaking, eating, and sharing the joys and pains of everyday life.[1]

(opposite)
Detail of *Jesus' disappearance in Emmaus.* Cambridge, Fitzwilliam Museum

Jesus calls Mary by name he speaks to her entire being. She realizes that the one who knows her most deeply is not moving away from her, but is coming to her offering her his unconditional love.

Her response is "Rabboni," "Master." I hear her response as her desire to have Jesus truly be her master, the master of her whole being: her thoughts and feelings, her passion and hope, even her most hidden emotions. I hear her say, "You who know me so fully, come and be my master. I do not want to keep you away from any part of myself. I want you to touch the deepest places of my heart so that I won't belong to anyone but you."

I can see what a healing moment this encounter must have been. Mary feels at once fully known and fully loved. The division between what she feels safe to show and what she does not dare to reveal no longer exists. She is fully seen and she knows that the eyes that see her are the eyes of forgiveness, mercy, love, and unconditional acceptance.

I sense that here, in this simple encounter, we can see a true religious moment. All fear is gone, and all has become love. And how better can this be expressed than by Jesus' words, "go and find my brothers, and tell them: I am ascending to my Father and your Father, to my God and your God" (John 20:17). There is no longer any difference between Jesus and those whom he loves. They are part of the intimacy that Jesus enjoys with his Father. They belong to the same family. They share the same life in God.

What a joy to be fully known and fully loved at the same time! It is the joy of belonging through Jesus to God and being there, fully safe and fully free.[2]

The Appearance by the Sea

When it was already light, there stood Jesus on the shore, though the disciples did not realize it was Jesus. Jesus called out, "Haven't you caught anything, friends?" And when they answered, "No," he said, "Throw the net out to starboard and you'll find something." So they threw the net out and could not haul it in because of the quantity of the fish. The disciple whom Jesus loved said to Peter, "It is the Lord." At these words, "It is the Lord," Simon Peter tied his outer garment around him (for he had nothing on) and jumped into the water. The other disciples came on in the boat, towing the net with the fish; they were only about a hundred yards from land.

—*John 21:4-8*

Even the Resurrection Is Hidden

What is most striking about the resurrection stories is that the resurrection of Jesus is described as a hidden event. When we speak about the hidden life of Jesus we have to go far beyond his years at Nazareth. The great mystery of Jesus' life is that all of it has a hidden quality. First of all, his conception and birth, then his many years living in obedience to his parents, then his so-called public life in which he kept asking those he cured not to speak about their healing, then his death outside the walls of Jerusalem between two criminals, and finally also his resurrection. Indeed, the resurrection of Jesus is not a glorious victory over his enemy. It is not a proof of his powers. It is not an argument against those who condemned him to death. Jesus did not appear to Annas, Caiaphas, Herod or Pilate, not even to his doubtful followers Nicodemus and Joseph of Arimathaea. There is no gesture of "being right after all." There is no "I always told you so." There isn't even a smile of satisfaction.

Today I was thinking how nobody recognizes Jesus immediately. They think he is the gardener, a stranger, or a ghost. But when a familiar gesture is there again—breaking bread, inviting the disciples to try for another catch, calling them by name—his friends know he is there with them. Absence and presence are touching each other. The old Jesus is gone. They no longer can be with him as before. The new Jesus, the risen Lord, is there, intimately, more intimately than ever.[3]

"You believe because you can see me. Blessed are those who have not seen and yet believe."

—John 20:29

Detail of *Jesus' disappearance in Emmaus*

No, the most decisive event in the history of creation is a deeply hidden event. Jesus appears as a stranger. Mary of Magdala sees a stranger in the garden. Cleopas and his friend find themselves walking with a stranger to Emmaus. The disciples see a stranger coming and think it is a ghost, and Peter, Thomas, Nathaniel, John, James and two other disciples hear a stranger calling out to them from the shore of a lake. How much of a stranger Jesus remains is succinctly expressed in that mysterious moment around the charcoal fire when Jesus offers bread and fish to his friends. John the Evangelist writes, "None of the disciples was bold enough to ask, 'Who are you?' They knew quite well it was the Lord" (John 21:12). Nowhere better than in this sentence is expressed the hiddenness of Jesus' resurrection. They knew who was giving them bread and fish, but didn't dare ask who he was. The difference between knowing and not knowing, presence and absence, revealing and hiding, have been transcended in the presence of the risen Lord.[4]

The Encounter at Emmaus

Now that very same day, two of them were on their way to a village called Emmaus, seven miles from Jerusalem, and they were talking together about all that had happened. And it happened that as they were talking together and discussing it, Jesus himself came up and walked by their side, but their eyes were prevented from recognizing him. —Luke 24:13-6

Tasting Death and Tasting Life

They were going home, disillusioned, dejected and downcast. We don't know much about these two friends, but Luke in his Gospel intimates quite clearly how they felt: beaten and oppressed. For a long time past, the Romans had been masters in their country; there was little genuine freedom and, as anyone would be, they were impatient to be free. When they came to know Jesus, their hopes were raised that this man from Nazareth would be able to give them the freedom they had been looking forward to for so long. But it had all come to nothing. The Jesus of whom they had expected so much had been arrested, condemned to death, and crucified by the Romans. Everything was just as it had been before: a life in which you could be picked up at any moment and put in jail. Again, freedom had not come. Cleopas and his friend had lost heart. In their despair they were making their way back home. It was not a way of hope. It was a cheerless way, a despairing way.

Jesus falls in with the two men, but they fail to recognize him. What does he do? First he listens to their sorry tale. He tags on to them in a very personal, you might say intimate, fashion. He enters right into their sense of disappointment. He shares their feelings with them. He is prepared to be where they are.

Here you have to imagine what had happened to Jesus

. . . All these discoveries gradually broke down many fences that had given me a safe garden and made me deeply aware that God's covenant with God's people includes everyone. For me personally, it was a time of searching, questioning, and agonizing, a time that was extremely lonely and not without moments of great inner uncertainty and ambiguity. The Jesus that I had come to know in my youth had died. I was traveling in a downcast way to Emmaus, and started hearing the Voice of someone who had joined me on the journey.[5]

himself. He had been hideously tortured to death and then buried. People often talk about Jesus as though his death had been followed immediately by his resurrection, but that's not what is reported to us by the Gospels. Jesus lay in the tomb for three days. That means not only that he had been like many people today the victim of oppression, but also that his body like everyone else's proceeded to decay. Whatever we do or say, however learned we are, however many our friends or great our wealth, soon—in ten, thirty, fifty, seventy years' time—we shall rot. Despair is our inner conviction that, in the end, it is utterly impossible to stop anything from coming to nothing.

Left with the impression that their great expectations had once again been shattered, Cleopas and his friend were grief-stricken. Yet again, it had become painfully clear to them just how meaningless their lives really were. They had already caught a whiff of the decay afflicting their own lives. So it was with bowed heads that they were making for home. It wasn't just their adventure with Jesus that was over, everything else had come to nothing in the end.

So when Jesus falls in with these two dejected men, he knows very well what is in their hearts. He knows from experience what human despair is. He knows death and the tomb; he knows what it means to be mortal. Cleopas and his friend must, I think, have perceived that this stranger was really no stranger at all. He understood them too well to remain strange to them for long. They saw that this man was not going to offer them easy words of comfort.

What does Jesus tell them? Not that death and the dissolution of life are unreal. Nor that their yearning for freedom is unreal. No: in what he says he takes seriously not only death and dissolution but their longing for freedom as well. He tells them that the Jesus on whom they had pinned all their hopes, the Jesus who was indeed dead and buried, this Jesus is alive. He tells them that for the Jesus whom they had admired so much, death and dissolution have become the way to liberation. And he says this in such a way that they sense in their innermost selves that his way can become their way too.

As Jesus was talking to them, they experienced in their hearts something new. It was as if their hearts were burning with a flame that came not from without but from within. Jesus had kindled in them something for which they had no words but which was so authentic, so real, that it overcame their depression. Jesus had not said: "It isn't nearly as bad as you think." He had said something entirely new: "The most tragic, the most painful, the most hopeless circumstances can become the way to the liberation you long for most of all."

It's very difficult for you and me to grasp much of this. In fact, it goes against logic. You and I as rational people say: "Death is death. Death and all that approaches it or leads to it must be avoided at all costs. The further away we can stay from death and everything connected to it—pain, illness, war, oppression, poverty, hunger and so on—the better for us." That's a normal, spontaneous human attitude. Jesus makes us see human existence from a quite different angle, one that is beyond the reach of our ordinary common sense.

Jesus makes us see existence in terms of his own experience that life is stronger and greater than death and dissolution. It's only with our hearts that we can understand this, and Luke doesn't write: "Then it dawned on them" or "Then they saw the light." No, he says: "Their hearts burned within them." The burning heart revealed something completely new to Cleopas and his friend. At the center of their being, of their humanity, something was generated that could disarm death and rob despair of its power; something much more than a new outlook on things, a new confidence or a new joy in living; something that can be described only as a new life or a new spirit. Nowadays we would say: "in their hearts the spiritual life had begun"; but it's better not to use these terms at this point. Otherwise, we shall stray too far from the actual story and there's too much still to be told.

They set out that instant and returned to Jerusalem. There they found the Eleven assembled together with their companions, who said to them, "The Lord has indeed risen and has appeared to Simon." Then they told their story of what had happened on the road and how they had recognized him at the breaking of bread.—Luke 24:33-5

When the three men reached Emmaus, so much had happened between them that the two companions were unwilling to let the stranger go. Between these two and Jesus there had arisen a bond which had given them new hope, even though they scarcely knew why. They felt that this unknown individual had given them something new. They didn't want to go indoors without him. So they said: "Stay with us. It's just about evening; and the day is as good as over." Luke, in his account, even says that they implored him to be their guest. Jesus accepted the invitation and went in with them.

And now there happens something which, for you and me, is of major significance. It touches the very core of the spiritual life. When they sit down to eat, Jesus takes some bread, speaks a blessing over it, and breaks it and offers it to them. And as he does so, they know suddenly and with unshakeable certainty that this stranger is Jesus, the same Jesus who had been put to death and laid in a tomb. But at the precise moment this certainty is given to them, he becomes invisible to them.

So much is going on here that it's difficult to get its full significance across to you, and so I shall limit myself to what is, for me, a very crucial aspect of this incident. What matters here is that the moment Cleopas and his friend recognized Jesus in the breaking of bread, his bodily presence was no longer required as a condition for their new hope. You might say that the bond between them and the stranger had become so intimate that everything strange about him vanishes. So close does he come to them that they no longer need a bodily manifestation in order to hope. They realize now that the new life born in them as they talked with him on the road will stay with them and give them the strength to return to Jerusalem and tell the other people why it isn't true that "it's all over." That's why Luke reports that they went off straightaway to tell Jesus' other friends about their experience.

Are you beginning to see what I'm getting at? Cleopas and his friend had become different people.[6]

Jesus Questions Peter

Jesus then stepped forward, took the bread and gave it to them, and the same with the fish. This was the third time that Jesus revealed himself to the disciples after rising from the dead. When they had eaten, Jesus said to Simon Peter, "Simon, son of John, do you love me more than these others do?" He answered, "Yes Lord, you know I love you." Jesus said to him, "Feed my lambs."

—John 21:13-5

Do You Know the Heart of God?

Before Jesus commissioned Peter to be a shepherd he asked him, "Simon, son of John, do you love me more than these others do?" He asked him again, "Do you love me?" And a third time he asked, "Do you love me?" We have to hear that question as being central to all of our Christian ministry because it is the question that can allow us to be, at the same time, irrelevant and totally self-confident.

Look at Jesus. The world did not pay any attention to him. He was crucified and put away. His message of love was rejected by a world in search of power, efficiency, and control. But there he was, appearing with wounds in his glorified body to a few friends who had eyes to see, ears to hear, and hearts to understand. This rejected, unknown, wounded Jesus simply asked, "Do you love me, do you really love me?" He whose only concern had been to announce the unconditional love of God had only one question to ask, "Do you love me?"

The question is not: How many people take you seriously? How much are you going to accomplish? Can you show some results? But: Are you in love with Jesus? Perhaps another way of putting the question would be: Do you know the incarnate God? In our world of loneliness and despair, there is an enormous need for men and women

God, you could say, is waiting for our answer. In a very mysterious way, God is dependent on us. God is saying, "I want to be vulnerable, I need your love. I have a desire for your affirmation of my love." God is a jealous God in the sense of wanting our love and wanting us to say yes. That's why in the end of the Gospel of John, Jesus asks Peter three times, "Do you love me?" God is waiting for us to respond. Life gives us endless opportunities for that response.[7]

who know the heart of God, a heart that forgives, that cares, that reaches out and wants to heal. In that heart there is no suspicion, no vindictiveness, no resentment, and not a tinge of hatred. It is a heart that wants only to give love and receive love in response. It is a heart that suffers immensely because it sees the magnitude of human pain and the great resistance to trusting the heart of God who wants to offer consolation and hope.

The Christian leader of the future is the one who truly knows the heart of God as it has become flesh, "a heart of flesh," in Jesus. Knowing God's heart means consistently, radically, and very concretely to announce and reveal that God is love and only love, and that every time fear, isolation, or despair begin to invade the human soul this is not something that comes from God. This sounds very simple and maybe even trite, but very few people know that they are loved without any conditions or limits.[8]

Others Will Lead You

In all truth I tell you, when you were young, you put on your own belt and walked where you liked; but when you grow old, you will stretch out your hands, and somebody else will put a belt round you and take you where you would rather not go.

—John 21:18

Am I ready to make that journey? Am I willing to let go of whatever power I have left, to unclench my fists and trust in the grace hidden in complete powerlessness? I don't know. I really don't know.[9]

Accepting New Levels of Vulnerability and Uncertainty

These words are the words that made it possible for me to move from Harvard to L'Arche. They touch the core of Christian leadership and are spoken to offer us ever and again new ways to let go of power and follow the humble way of Jesus. The world says, "When you were young you were dependent and could not go where you wanted, but when you grow old you will be able to make your own decisions, go your own way, and control your own destiny." But Jesus has a different vision of maturity: It is the ability and willingness to be led where you would rather not go.

Immediately after Peter has been commissioned to be a leader of his sheep, Jesus confronts him with the hard truth that the servant-leader is the leader who is being led to unknown, undesirable, and painful places. The way of the Christian leader is not the way of upward mobility in which our world has invested so much, but the way of downward mobility ending on the cross. This might sound morbid and masochistic, but for those who have heard the voice of the first love and said "yes" to it, the downward-moving way of Jesus is the way of the joy and the peace of God, a joy and peace that is not of this world.

Here we touch the most important quality of Christian leadership in the future. It is not a leadership of power and control, but a leadership of powerlessness and humility in which the suffering servant of God, Jesus Christ, is made manifest. I, obviously, am not speaking about a psycholog-

In these words he indicated the kind of death by which Peter would give glory to God. After this he said, "Follow me."—John 21:19

ically weak leadership in which the Christian leader is simply the passive victim of the manipulations of his milieu. No, I am speaking of a leadership in which power is constantly abandoned in favor of love. It is a true spiritual leadership. Powerlessness and humility in the spiritual life do not refer to people who have no spine and who let everyone else make decisions for them. They refer to people who are so deeply in love with Jesus that they are ready to follow him wherever he guides them, always trusting that, with him, they will find life and find it abundantly.[10]

All of Humanity Is Included

The eleven disciples set out for Galilee, to the mountain where Jesus had arranged to meet them. When they saw him they fell down before him, though some hesitated. Jesus came and spoke to them. He said, "All authority in heaven and on earth has been given to me. Go, therefore, make disciples of all nations; baptize them in the name of the Father and of the Son and of the Holy Spirit, and teach them to observe all the commands I gave you. And look, I am with you always; yes, to the end of time."

—Matthew 28:16-20

Jesus Includes More Than He Excludes

Jesus says, "Whoever is not with me is against me, and whoever does not gather with me scatters" (Luke 11:23). These words frighten me. I want to be with Jesus, but often it feels like I want to be with many others too! There is within me a strong tendency to play it safe. I want to stay friends with everyone. I do not like conflict or controversy. I hate divisions and confrontations among people. Is this a weakness, a lack of courage to speak out forcefully, a fear of rejection, a preoccupation with being liked? Or is it a strength that allows me to bring people together and be reconciled, to create community, and to build bridges?

Jesus also says, "Do you think that I have come to bring peace to the earth? No, I tell you, but rather division! From now on, five in one household will be divided, three against two and two against three" (Luke 12:51-2). What do I do with all these harsh words? Isn't there enough religious conflict? Isn't Jesus inciting me here to a confrontational life and stirring me up to create separation between people? I still remember Pasolini's movie The Gospel According to St. Matthew. There Jesus is portrayed as an intense, angry rebel who alienates everyone in sight.

Jesus lived in a very particular territory and time, with very particular people. But through his death he broke out of the boundaries of time and place. He became for all people the Jesus who came to make a covenant with humanity, made visible through his death. "When I die, I can send my Spirit and the Spirit will blow where it wants." That's the mystery of the cross, that place from which all the energy bursts forth and Jesus becomes the lover of all people.[11]

I have made an inner decision to keep looking at Jesus as the one who calls us to the heart of God, a heart that knows only love. It is from that perspective that I reflect on everything Jesus says, including his harsh statements. Jesus created divisions, but I have chosen to believe that these divisions were the result not of intolerance or fanaticism but of his radical call to love, forgive, and be reconciled.

Every time I have an opportunity to create understanding between people and foster moments of healing, forgiving, and uniting, I will try to do it, even though I might be criticized as too soft, too bending, too appeasing. Is this desire a lack of fervor and zeal for the truth? Is it an unwillingness to be a martyr? Is it spinelessness? I am not always sure what comes from my weakness and what comes from my strength. Probably I will never know. But I have to trust that, after sixty-four years of life, I have some ground to stand on, a ground where Jesus stands with me.[12]

The Mission Is Real

Each one of us has a mission in life. Jesus prays to his Father for his followers, saying, "As you sent me into the world, I have sent them in to the world" (John 17:18).

We seldom realize fully that we have to choose how, where and with whom to live. We act as if we were simply dropped down in creation and have to decide how to entertain ourselves until we die. But we were sent into the world by God, just as Jesus was. Once we start living our lives with that conviction, we will soon know what we were sent to do.[13]

Spiritual Fire

When Pentecost day came round, they had all met together, when suddenly there came from heaven a sound as of a violent wind which filled the entire house in which they were sitting; and there appeared to them tongues as of fire; these separated and came to rest on the head of each of them. They were all filled with the Holy Spirit and began to speak different languages as the Spirit gave them power to express themselves.

—Acts 2:1-4

The Spirit Actualizes Our Faith

We are waiting for the Spirit to come. Are we really? This morning during the Eucharist I spoke a little about preparing ourselves for Pentecost just as we prepare ourselves for Christmas and Easter. Still, for most of us, Pentecost is a nonevent. While on secular calendars Christmas and Easter are still marked, Pentecost is spectacularly absent.

But Pentecost is the coming of the Spirit of Jesus into the world. It is the celebration of God breaking through the boundaries of time and space and opening the whole world for the re-creating power of love. Pentecost is freedom, the freedom of the Spirit to blow where it wants.

Without Pentecost the Christ-event—the life, death, and resurrection of Jesus—remains imprisoned in history as something to remember, think about, and reflect on. The Spirit of Jesus comes to dwell within us, so that we can become living Christs here and now. Pentecost lifts the whole mystery of salvation out of its particularities and makes it into something universal, embracing all peoples, all countries, all seasons, and all eras. Pentecost is also the moment of empowering. Each individual human being can claim the Spirit of Jesus as the guiding spirit of his or her

*"Unless I go
the Paraclete [the Spirit] will
not come to you;
but if I do go,
I will send him to you.
He will lead you to the
complete truth."*

—John 16:7, 13

With these words Jesus points forward to the new life in the Spirit that will be revealed at Pentecost. It will be a life lived in "complete truth." Closely related to the word "betrothal," the "complete truth" means full intimacy with God, a betrothal in which the complete divine life is given to us.[14]

life. In that Spirit we can speak and act freely and confidently with the knowledge that the same Spirit that inspired Jesus is inspiring us.

We certainly have to prepare ourselves carefully for this feast so that we can not only receive fully the gifts of the Spirit but also let the Spirit bear fruit within us.[15]

A Prayer at Pentecost

Dear Lord, listen to my prayer. You promised your disciples that you would not leave them alone but would send the Holy Spirit to guide them and lead them to the full Truth.

I feel like I am groping in the dark. I have received much from you, and still it is hard for me simply to be quiet and present in your presence. My mind is so chaotic, so full of dispersed ideas, plans, memories, and fantasies. I want to be with you and you alone, concentrate on your Word, listen to your voice, and look at you as you reveal yourself to your friends. But even with the best intentions I wander off to less important things and discover that my heart is drawn to my own little worthless treasures.

I cannot pray without the power from on high, the power of your Spirit. Send your Spirit, Lord, so that your Spirit can pray in me, can say "Lord Jesus," and can call out "Abba, Father."

I am waiting, Lord, I am expecting, I am hoping. Do not leave me without your Spirit. Give me your unifying and consoling Spirit. Amen.[16]

"He Will Come Again"

And while he was sitting on the Mount of Olives the disciples came and asked him when they were by themselves, "Tell us, when is this going to happen, and what sign will there be of your coming and the end of the world?" And Jesus answered them, "Take care that no one deceives you, because many will come using my name and saying, 'I am the Christ,' and they will deceive many. You will hear of wars and rumors of wars; see that you are not alarmed, for this is something that must happen, but the end will not be yet."

—Matthew 24:3-6

Jesus came in the fullness of time. He will come again in the fullness of time. Wherever Jesus, the Christ is, time is brought to its fullness.[17]

A Forgotten Question

The coming again of Christ is his coming in judgment. The question that will sound through the heavens and the earth will be the question that we always tend to remain deaf to. Our lives as we live them seem lives that anticipate questions that never will be asked. It seems as if we are getting ourselves ready for the question, "How much did you earn during your lifetime?" or, "How many friends did you make?" or, "How much progress did you make on your career?" or, "How much influence did you have on people?" Were any of these to be the questions Christ will ask when he comes again in glory, many of us could approach the judgment day with great confidence.

But nobody is going to hear any of these questions. The question we all are going to face is the question we are least prepared for. It is the question: "What have you done for the least of mine?"

It is the question of the just judge who in that question reveals to us that making peace and working for justice can never be separated. As long as there are people who are less than we, in whatever way or form, the question of the last judgment will be with us. As long as there are strangers, hungry, naked, and sick people; prisoners, refugees, and slaves, people who are handicapped physically, mentally, or emotionally, people without work, a home, or a piece of land, there will be that haunting question from the throne of judgment: "What have you done for the least of mine?" The question makes the coming of Christ an ever present event.[18]

Eyes to See

The spiritual knowledge that we belong to God and are safe with God even as we live in a very destructive world allows us to see in the midst of all the turmoil, fear, and agony of history "the Son of Man coming in a cloud with power and great glory" (Luke 21:27). Even though Jesus speaks about this as about a final event, it is not just one more thing that is going to happen after all the terrible things are over. Just as the end time is already here, so too is the coming of the Son of Man. It is an event in the realm of the Spirit and thus not subject to the boundaries of time.

Those who live in communion with Jesus have the eyes to see and the ears to hear the second coming of Jesus among them in the here and now. Jesus says, "Before this generation has passed away all will have taken place" (Luke 21:32). And this is true for each faithful generation.[19]

❧ Jesus, A Gospel ❧

Conclusion

"All I have is yours and all you have is mine . . . I am no longer in the world, but they are in the world, and I am coming to you. Holy Father, keep those you have given me true to your name, so they may be one like us."

—John 17:10-1

Jesus' whole being is perpetual seeing of the Father. Jesus' life and works are an uninterrupted contemplation of his Father.[1]

Jesus' Life

There is little doubt that Jesus' life was a very busy life. He was busy teaching his disciples, preaching to the crowds, healing the sick, exorcising demons, responding to questions from foes and friends, and moving from one place to another. Jesus was so involved in activities that it became difficult to have any time alone. The following story gives us the picture: "They brought to him all who were sick and those who were possessed by devils. The whole town came crowding round the door, and he cured many who were suffering from diseases of one kind or another; he also cast out many devils . . . In the morning, long before dawn, he got up and left the house, and went off to a lonely place and prayed there. Simon and his companions set out in search of him, and when they found him they said, 'Everybody is looking for you.' He answered, 'Let us go elsewhere, to the neighboring country towns, so that I can preach there too, because that is why I came.' And he went all through Galilee, preaching in their synagogues and casting out devils" (Mark 1:32-9).

It is clear from this account that Jesus had a very filled life and was seldom if ever left alone. He might even appear to us as a fanatic driven by a compulsion to get his message across at any cost. The truth, however, is different. The deeper we enter into the Gospel accounts of his life, the more we see that Jesus was not a zealot trying to accomplish many different things in order to reach a self-

"In all truth I tell you, you will be weeping and wailing while the world will rejoice; you will be sorrowful, but your sorrow will turn to joy. A woman in childbirth suffers, because her time has come; but when she has given birth to the child she forgets the suffering in her joy that a human being has been born into the world. So it is with you: you are sad now, but I shall see you again, and your hearts will be full of joy, and that joy no one shall take from you."—John 16:20-2

imposed goal. On the contrary, everything we know about Jesus indicates that he was concerned with only one thing: to do the will of his Father. Nothing in the Gospels is as impressive as Jesus' single-minded obedience to his Father. From his first recorded words in the Temple, "Did you not know that I must be busy with my Father's affairs?" (Luke 2:49), to his last words on the cross, "Father, into your hands I commit my spirit" (Luke 23:46), Jesus' only concern was to do the will of his Father. He says, "The Son can do nothing by himself; he can do only what he sees the Father doing" (John 5:19). The works Jesus did are the works the Father sent him to do, and the words he spoke are the words the Father gave him. He leaves no doubt about this: "If I am not doing my Father's work, there is no need to believe me . . ." (John 10:37); "My word is not my own; it is the word of the one who sent me" (John 14:24).

Jesus is not our Savior simply because of what he said to us or did for us. He is our Savior because what he said and did was said and done in obedience to his Father. That is why St. Paul could say, "As by one man's disobedience many were made sinners, so by one man's obedience many will be made righteous" (Romans 5:19). Jesus is the obedient one. The center of his life is this obedient relationship with the Father. This may be hard for us to understand, because the word obedience has so many negative connotations in our society. It makes us think of authority figures who impose their wills against our desires. It makes us remember unhappy childhood events or hard tasks performed under threats of punishment. But none of this applies to Jesus' obedience. His obedience means a total, fearless listening to his loving Father. Between the Father and the Son there is only love. Everything that belongs to the Father, he entrusts to the Son (Luke 10:22), and everything the Son received, he returns to the Father. The Father opens himself totally to the Son and puts everything in his hands: all knowledge (John 12:50), all glory (John 8:54), all power (John 5:19-21). And the Son opens himself totally to the Father and thus returns everything into his Father's hands. "I came from the Father and have come into the world and now I leave the world to go to the Father" (John 16:28).

This inexhaustible love between the Father and the Son includes and yet transcends all forms of love known to us. It includes the love of a father and mother, a brother and sister, a husband and wife, a teacher and friend. But it also goes far beyond the many limited and limiting human experiences of love we know. It is a caring yet demanding love. It is a supportive yet severe love. It is a gentle yet strong love. It is a love that gives life yet accepts death. In this divine love Jesus was sent into the world, to this divine love Jesus offered himself on the cross. This all-embracing love, which epitomizes the relationship between the Father and the Son, is a divine Person, coequal with the Father and the Son. It has a personal name. It is called the Holy Spirit. The Father loves the Son and pours himself out in the Son. The Son is loved by the Father and returns all he is to the Father. The Spirit is love itself, eternally embracing the Father and the Son.

This eternal community of love is the center and source of Jesus' spiritual life, a life of uninterrupted attentiveness to the Father in the Spirit of love. It is from this life that Jesus' ministry grows. His eating and fasting, his praying and acting, his traveling and his preaching and teaching, his exorcising and healing, were all done in this Spirit of love. We will never understand the full meaning of Jesus' richly varied ministry unless we see how the many things are rooted in the one thing: listening to the Father in the intimacy of perfect love. When we see this, we will also realize that the goal of Jesus' ministry is nothing less than to bring us into this most intimate community.

Our Lives

Our lives are destined to become like the life of Jesus. The whole purpose of Jesus' ministry is to bring us to the house of his Father. Not only did Jesus come to free us from the bonds of sin and death, he also came to lead us into the intimacy of his divine life. It is difficult for us to imagine what this means; we tend to emphasize the distance between Jesus and ourselves. We see Jesus as the all-knowing and all-powerful Son of God who is unreachable for us sinful, broken human beings. But in thinking this way, we forget that Jesus came to give us his own life. He came to lift us up into loving community with the Father. Only when we recognize the radical purpose of Jesus' ministry will we be able to understand the meaning of the spiritual life. Everything that belongs to Jesus is given for us to receive. All that Jesus does we may also do. Jesus does not speak about us as second-class citizens. He does not withhold anything from us: "I have made known to you everything I have learned from my Father" (John 15:15); "Whoever believes in me will perform the same works as I do myself" (John 14:12). Jesus wants us to be where he is. In his priestly prayer, he leaves no doubt about his intentions: "Father, may they be one in us, as you are in me and I am in you . . . I have given them the glory you gave to me, that they may be one as we are one. With me in them and you in me, may they be so completely one that the world will realize . . . that I have loved them as much as you loved me. Father, I want those you have given me to be with me where I am, so that they may always see the glory you have given me . . . I have made your name known to them and will continue to make it known, so that the love with which you loved me may be in them, and so that I may be in them" (John 17:21-6).

These words beautifully express the nature of Jesus' ministry. He became like us so that we might become like him. He did not cling to his equality with God, but emptied himself and became as we are so that we might become like him and thus share in his divine life.

This radical transformation of our lives is the work of the Holy Spirit. The disciples could hardly comprehend what Jesus meant. As long as Jesus was present to them in the flesh, they did not yet recognize his full presence in the Spirit. That is why Jesus said: "It is for your own good that I am going, because, unless I go, the Advocate [the Holy Spirit] will not come to you; but if I do go, I will send him to you . . . When the Spirit of truth comes he will lead you to the complete truth, since he will not be speaking as from himself but will say only what he has learned; and he will tell you of the things to come. He will glorify me, since all he tells you will be taken from what is mine. Everything the Father has is mine; that is why I said: All he tells you will be taken from what is mine" (John 16:7, 13-5).

Jesus sends the Spirit so that we may be led to the full truth of the divine life. Truth does not mean an idea, concept, or doctrine, but the true relationship. To be led into the truth is to be led into the same relationship that Jesus has with the Father; it is to enter into a divine betrothal.

Thus Pentecost is the completion of Jesus' mission. On Pentecost the fullness of Jesus' ministry becomes visible. When the Holy Spirit descends upon the disciples and dwells with them, their lives are transformed into Christ-like lives, lives shaped by the same love that exists between the Father and the Son. The spiritual life is indeed a life in which we are lifted up to become partakers of the divine life.

To be lifted up into the divine life of the Father, the Son, and the Holy Spirit does not mean, however, to be taken out of the world. On the contrary, those who have entered into the spiritual life are precisely the ones who are sent into the world to continue and fulfill the work that Jesus began. The spiritual life does not remove us from the world but leads us deeper into it. Jesus says to his Father, "As you sent me into the world, I have sent them into the world" (John 17:18). He makes it clear that precisely because his disciples no longer belong to the world, they can live in the world as he did: "I am not asking you to remove them from the world, but to protect them from the evil one. They do not belong to the world any more than I belong to the world" (John 17:15-6). Life in the Spirit of Jesus is therefore a life in which Jesus' coming into the world—his incarnation, his death, and resurrection—is lived out by those who

"I have told you all this so that you may find peace in me. In the world you will have hardship, but be courageous: I have conquered the world."

—*John 16:33*

"Holy Father, keep those you have given me true to your name, so that they may be one like us. While I was with them, I kept those you had given me true to your name. I have watched over them and not one is lost . . . But now I am coming to you and I say these things in the world to share my joy with them to the full. I passed your word on to them, and the world hated them, becasue they belong to the world no more than I belong to the world . . . Consecrate them in the truth; your word is truth. As you sent me into the world, I have sent them into the world, and for their sake I consecrate myself so that they too may be consecrated in truth."
—John 17:11-4, 17-9

have entered into the same obedient relationship to the Father which marked Jesus' own life. Having become sons and daughters as Jesus was Son, our lives become a continuation of Jesus' mission.

"Being in the world without being of the world." These words summarize well the way Jesus speaks of the spiritual life. It is a life in which we are totally transformed by the Spirit of love. Yet it is a life in which everything seems to remain the same. To live a spiritual life does not mean that we must leave our families, give up our jobs, or change our ways of working; it does not mean that we have to withdraw from social or political activities, or lose interest in literature and art; it does not require severe forms of asceticism or long hours of prayer. Changes such as these may in fact grow out of our spiritual life, and for some people radical decisions may be necessary. But the spiritual life can be lived in as many ways as there are people. What is new is that we have moved from the many things to the kingdom of God. What is new is that we are set free from the compulsions of our world and have set our hearts on the only necessary thing. What is new is that we no longer experience the many things, people, and events as endless causes for worry, but begin to experience them as the rich variety of ways in which God makes his presence known to us.

Indeed, living a spiritual life requires a change of heart, a conversion. Such a conversion may be marked by a sudden inner change, or it can take place through a long, quiet process of transformation. But it always involves an inner experience of oneness. We realize that we are in the center, and that from there all that is and all that takes place can be seen and understood as part of the mystery of God's life with us. Our conflicts and pains, our tasks and promises, our families and friends, our activities and projects, our hopes and aspirations, no longer appear to us as a fatiguing variety of things which we can barely keep together, but rather as affirmations and revelations of the new life of the Spirit in us. "All these other things," which so occupied and preoccupied us, now come as gifts or challenges that strengthen and deepen the new life which we have discovered. This does not mean that the spiritual life makes things easier or takes our struggles and pains away. The lives of Jesus' disciples clearly show that suffering does not diminish because of conversion. Sometimes it even becomes more intense. But our attention is no longer directed to the "more or less." What matters is to listen attentively to the Spirit and to go obediently where we are being led, whether to a joyful or a painful place.

Poverty, pain, struggle, anguish, agony, and even inner darkness may continue to be part of our experience. They may even be God's way of purifying us. But life is no longer boring, resentful, depressing, or lonely because we have come to know that everything that happens is part of our way to the house of the Father.[2]

Notes

God's Way

1 *The Road to Daybreak*, 227, adapted
2 *Letters to Marc about Jesus*, 7
3 *Lifesigns*, 20-1, adapted
4 *Letters to Marc about Jesus*, 72
5 *Lifesigns*, 66-7
6 *Introduction to the Spiritual Life*,
    Harvard University, 1983, Handout 14
7 *Letters to Marc about Jesus*, 44-5
8 *Letters to Marc about Jesus*, 41-2, adapted
9 *The Road to Daybreak*, 154
10 *Here and Now*, 32-3
11 *Letters to Marc about Jesus*, 59-61, adapted
12 *The Life of the Beloved*, 104

The Gospel Begins

1 *Seeds of Hope*, 165
2 *The Road to Daybreak*, 91-2, adapted
3 *Seeds of Hope*, 165-6
4 *The Inner Voice of Love*, 57
5 *The Road to Daybreak*, 100-1, adapted
6 *The Road to Daybreak*, 150
7 *The Road to Peace*, 219-20, adapted
8 *Introduction to the Spiritual Life*,
    Harvard University, 1983, Handout 14
9 *Adam: God's Beloved*, 32
10 *The Life of the Beloved*, 38
11 *The Road to Daybreak*, 118
12 *Parting Words*, 8-10, adapted

Reaching Out

1 *Bread for the Journey*, May 20
2 *The Inner Voice of Love*, 40-1, adapted
3 *With Burning Hearts*, 46-8
4 *With Burning Hearts*, 82
5 *Sabbatical Journey*, 130-1
6 *Sabbatical Journey*, 208-9, adapted
7 *The Road to Daybreak*, 222
8 *The Road to Daybreak*, 147-8
9 *The Only Necessary Thing*, 201
10 *The Road to Peace*, 14-5
11 *Lifesigns*, 36-7
12 *Sabbatical Journey*, 127, adapted
13 *Parting Words*, 13-5, adapted
14 *The Living Reminder*, 31
15 *Letters to Marc about Jesus*, 45-6
16 *Living the Beatitudes*, Foreword by Henri J. M.
    Nouwen, 5, adapted
17 *Letters to Marc about Jesus*, 54
18 *Reaching Out*, 73, adapted
19 *Here and Now*, 60-1
20 *Here and Now*, 120-1, adapted
21 *The Road to Peace*, 171
22 *Sabbatical Journey*, 129
23 *The Road to Peace*, 170-1
24 *The Road to Peace*, 157
25 *Here and Now*, 53-4
26 *Here and Now*, 89-93, adapted
27 *The Road to Daybreak*, 152-3
28 *Sabbatical Journey*, 128
29 *Reaching Out*, 62
30 *The Road to Daybreak*, 15
31 *The Road to Daybreak*, 16
32 *Sabbatical Journey*, 173
33 *The Road to Peace*, 65
34 *The Road to Daybreak*, 170-1
35 *With Burning Hearts*, 87
36 *In the Name of Jesus*, 40-2, adapted
37 *Behold the Beauty of the Lord*, 19
38 *Lifesigns*, 21-2
39 *The Road to Peace*, 58
40 *Here and Now*, 57
41 *Here and Now*, 55-6
42 *Here and Now*, 59-60, adapted
43 *The Road to Peace*, 131-2
44 *The Inner Voice of Love*, 41
45 *Lifesigns*, 59-60
46 *Lifesigns*, 18-20 adapted
47 *The Return of the Prodigal Son*, 48

48 *The Road to Daybreak*, 189-90
49 *The Road to Daybreak*, 193-4

Entering the Heart of the Gospel

1 *Letters to Marc about Jesus*, 83
2 *Sabbatical Journey*, 113
3 *Sabbatical Journey*, 211
4 *Letters to Marc about Jesus*, 29-30, adapted
5 *The Road to Daybreak*, 90-1
6 *The Return of the Prodigal Son*, 117, adapted
7 *Can You Drink the Cup?*, 93
8 *Can You Drink the Cup?*, 19-21, adapted
9 "Intimacy, Fecundity, Ecstasy," 23
10 "Intimacy, Fecundity, Ecstasy," 23
11 *Sabbatical Journey, 132-3*
12 *Bread for the Journey*, April 11-2
13 *The Road to Daybreak*, 134-5
14 *The Road to Daybreak*, 201-2, adapted
15 *Walk with Jesus*, 5
16 *The Road to Daybreak*, 158-60
17 *The Life of the Beloved*, 88
18 *With Burning Hearts*, 66-9
19 "A Spirituality of Waiting," *Weavings*, January 1987, 17
20 *The Road to Daybreak*, 155-6, adapted
21 *Reaching Out*, 89
22 *The Road to Daybreak*, 174-5
23 *Sabbatical Journey*, 165
24 *The Road to Daybreak*, 180-1, adapted

For This I Have Come

1 *A Cry for Mercy*, 7, adapted
2 *Can You Drink the Cup?*, 48-9
3 *Reaching Out*, 107-8, adapted
4 *The Road to Daybreak*, 120, adapted
5 *Adam: God's Beloved*, 83
6 "A Spirituality of Waiting," *Weavings*, January 1987, 15-6, adapted
7 *The Inner Voice of Love*, 93-4, adapted
8 *Walk with Jesus*, 9-11

9 *The Road to Peace*, 111
10 Translation adapted
11 *Walk with Jesus*, 16-7
12 *Walk with Jesus*, 35
13 *Walk with Jesus*, 34-5, adapted
14 *Letters to Marc about Jesus*, 63
15 *Walk with Jesus*, 69-70
16 *The Road to Daybreak*, 149-50
17 *Letters to Marc about Jesus*, 44-5
18 *Walk with Jesus*, 75-6
19 *Walk with Jesus*, 70
20 *The Road to Peace*, 111-2, adapted
21 *Seeds of Hope*, 182
22 *Walk with Jesus*, 87-9, adapted

Death and Darkness Are Overcome

1 *The Road to Peace*, 166, adapted
2 *The Road to Daybreak*, 164-5
3 *Sabbatical Journey*, 144
4 *The Road to Peace*, 162-3
5 *The Road to Peace*, xxii
6 *Letters to Marc about Jesus*, 12-6, adapted
7 *The Road to Peace*, 220
8 *In the Name of Jesus*, 23-5
9 *Our Greatest Gift*, 4
10 *In the Name of Jesus*, 61-4
11 *The Road to Peace*, 178, adapted
12 *Sabbatical Journey*, 126-7
13 *Bread for the Journey*, April 23
14 *Behold the Beauty of the Lord*, 63
15 *Sabbatical Journey*, 160-1
16 *The Only Necessary Thing*, 216
17 *Bread for the Journey*, December 18
18 *The Road to Peace*, 126, adapted
19 *Bread for the Journey*, September 16

Jesus, A Gospel

1 *Clowning in Rome*, 78
2 *Making All Things New*, 44-59

Sources

All titles are by Henri Nouwen, unless otherwise noted

Adam: God's Beloved (Maryknoll, N.Y.: Orbis, 1997)

Behold the Beauty of the Lord (Notre Dame: Ave Maria, 1987)

Bread for the Journey: Thoughts for Every Day of the Year (HarperSanFrancisco, 1996)

Can You Drink the Cup? The Challenge of the Spiritual Life (Notre Dame: Ave Maria, 1996)

Clowning in Rome: Reflections on Solitude, Celibacy, Prayer and Contemplation (New York: Doubleday, Image, 1979)

A Cry for Mercy: Prayers from the Genesee (New York: Doubleday, 1981)

Here and Now: Living in the Spirit (New York: Crossroad, 1994)

In the Name of Jesus: Reflections on Christian Leadership (New York: Crossroad, 1989)

The Inner Voice of Love: A Journey Through Anguish to Freedom (New York: Doubleday, 1996)

"Intimacy, Fecundity, Ecstasy," *Radix* (May/June, 1984), 8-23

Introduction to the Spiritual Life, Handout 14, from course at Harvard Divinity School; unpublished manuscript

Letters to Marc about Jesus (San Francisco: Harper and Row, 1988)

The Life of the Beloved: Spiritual Living in a Secular World (New York: Crossroad, 1992)

Lifesigns: Intimacy, Fecundity, and Ecstasy in Christian Perspective (New York: Doubleday, 1986)

The Living Reminder: Service and Prayer in Memory of Jesus Christ (San Francisco: Harper and Row, 1977)

Living the Beatitudes: Daily Reflections for Lent L'Arche Daybreak Community, Foreword by Henri J.M. Nouwen (Cincinnati: St. Anthony Messenger, 1989)

Making All Things New: An Invitation to the Spiritual Life (San Francisco: Harper and Row, 1981)

The Only Necessary Thing: Living a Prayerful Life (New York: Crossroad, 1999)

Our Greatest Gift: A Meditation on Dying and Caring (San Francisco: HarperCollins, 1994)

"Parting Words: A Conversation on Prayer with Henri Nouwen," interview by Rebecca Laird in *Sacred Journey:* The Journal of Fellowship in Prayer, no. 6; December, 1996)

Reaching Out: The Three Movements of the Spiritual Life (New York: Doubleday, 1975)

The Return of the Prodigal Son (New York: Doubleday, 1992)

The Road to Daybreak: A Spiritual Journey (New York: Doubleday, 1988)

The Road to Peace: Writings on Peace and Justice, John Dear, ed. (Maryknoll, N.Y.: Orbis, 1998)

Sabbatical Journey: The Final Year (New York: Crossroad, 1998)

Seeds of Hope: A Henri Nouwen Reader, Robert Durback, ed.; 2nd ed. (New York: Doubleday, Image, 1997)

"A Spirituality of Waiting," *Weavings* (Jan. 1987) 6-17

Walk With Jesus: Stations of the Cross (Maryknoll, N.Y.: Orbis, 1990)

With Burning Hearts: A Meditation on the Eucharistic Life (Maryknoll, N.Y.: Orbis, 1994)

Index of Biblical Passages